Teaching Notes on Piano Exam Pieces 2011 & 2012

Grades 1–7

TIMOTHY BARRATT
STEPHEN ELLIS
JULIAN HELLABY
MARGARET MURRAY McLEOD
ANTHONY WILLIAMS

Teaching Notes on Piano Exam Pieces 2011 & 2012

Grades 1–7

With an introduction by CLARA TAYLOR

ABRSM

First published in 2010 by
ABRSM (Publishing) Ltd, a wholly owned subsidiary of ABRSM

© 2010 by The Associated Board of the Royal Schools of Music

ISBN: 978 1 84849 231 8

AB 3574

A CIP catalogue for this book is available from The British Library.

Typeset by Hope Services (Abingdon) Ltd
Printed in England by Page Bros Ltd, Norwich

CONTENTS

NOTES ON CONTRIBUTORS

Timothy Barratt, ARAM GRSM LRAM ARCM LMusTCL, is a professor at the Royal Academy of Music and Head of Keyboard at Dulwich College, London. He has toured extensively and broadcast as a solo pianist, accompanist and chamber music player. He adjudicates, directs workshops for teachers and is an ABRSM examiner, trainer and consultant moderator, and a mentor for the Certificate of Teaching.

Stephen Ellis, Hon GRSM LRAM LGSM ARCM, studied piano and accompaniment at the Royal Academy of Music and has performed extensively in the UK and abroad. He is an experienced piano teacher of all levels, and as a vocal coach he has worked with many distinguished singers. He adjudicates and is an examiner, trainer, moderator and presenter for ABRSM, working internationally in most capacities.

Julian Hellaby, PhD MMus BMus LRAM ARAM, studied piano at the Royal Academy of Music and has performed throughout the UK and overseas. He is an ABRSM examiner, trainer, moderator and public presenter, as well as a mentor for the ABRSM's Certificate of Teaching course. He has extensive experience of piano teaching at all levels, and is currently Associate Senior Lecturer at Coventry University. He has released six CDs, and his book *Reading Musical Interpretation* was recently published by Ashgate.

Margaret Murray McLeod, ARAM FTCL LRAM ARCM, studied piano and composition at the Royal Academy of Music. As well as performing as a soloist and accompanist, she has many years' experience of teaching at all levels. From 1972 she trained student teachers and performers at Napier University, Edinburgh, where she was Senior Lecturer for Performance Studies until 1997. Her work as a lecturer, examiner and adjudicator has taken her worldwide.

Anthony Williams, MMus Dip.RAM GRSM LRAM, has an active performing, teaching and adjudicating career in the UK and abroad and is currently Head of Keyboard and Instrumental Music at Radley College, Oxfordshire. He is an examiner (jazz and classical), trainer and moderator for ABRSM as well as a mentor for the Certificate of Teaching. He is the compiler of *Fingerprints*, a collection of original repertoire for piano, and the *Best of Grade* series for piano, and editor of *Simply Classics* (all published by Faber Music).

INTRODUCTION

Teachers always enjoy sharing professional insights. The contributors to these *Teaching Notes* – all distinguished teachers as well as being examiners – are no exception. Their detailed investigation into the new syllabus will offer you essential guidance on how to prepare your pupils for their piano exam, and work towards achieving the best results.

The wide choice of repertoire for every grade gives the opportunity to match the pieces to the pupil. Sometimes you might choose a style that immediately suits, and at other times you might take a more medicinal approach in order to tackle shortcomings. There are obvious winners on the lists, which will appear many times in the exams, but do also explore the alternative pieces not published in the graded volumes. There are some delights to be found that may just be the answer for some pupils. The inclusion of arrangements continues to be a well-received attribute to the piano syllabus. We hope this will be beneficial in widening repertoire choices at the lower grades, and more importantly introduce young pianists to, and encourage their interest in, the wider world of other non-pianistic genres.

From Grade 1 to Grade 8 the three lists have more in common than you might expect. List A contains the technically demanding repertoire, List B the more warmly expressive pieces, and List C has a tremendous variety of styles, often with some jazzy rhythms. Despite the enormous difference in standards between Grade 1 and Grade 8, candidates' strengths and weaknesses tend to follow predictable paths in each list. It will be helpful, therefore, to consider the three lists in more detail.

LIST A

In List A, definition of fingerwork, clarity of articulation and control of co-ordination are necessary, as fluency increases through the grades. These technical challenges, especially runs and ornaments, can upset the basic rhythm, and in their determination some candidates use an over-emphatic heavy touch that is self-defeating. An ability to keep the hands in exact ensemble is needed. Examiners often hear hands starting together then parting company at difficult corners. In higher grades, part-playing will often be a feature in List A and it's fairly rare to hear this successfully achieved. Many candidates over-emphasize the subject without adjusting the balance of the other lines. When this happens, control of dynamics and phrasing is inevitably affected.

Ornaments can be simplified or omitted in the early grades if they are causing problems with the rhythm. A steady basic beat is a higher priority than the decorations. In later grades some ornamentation is often necessary and certainly needs to be included to achieve higher marks.

In their efforts to manage the technicalities, many candidates are less aware of the musical content of the List A pieces. It's a delight to hear the right texture, clear dynamics and musical phrasing capturing the elegant style of the repertoire, which often comes from quite an early era.

LIST B

List B gives every opportunity to show more expressive phrasing and tonal warmth. The pieces are selected mostly from the Classical or Romantic styles, and cantabile tone will be needed for the melodies. Phrasing comes right to the forefront and balance of hands needs real care, as these pieces often follow the pattern of right-hand melody and left-hand accompaniment. Pedalling will be necessary for the more legato choices, with clean, rhythmic legato pedalling requiring good physical co-ordination. Even in higher grades we frequently hear the hands and the right foot not really coinciding.

Rubato is a vital part of musical phrasing and is often needed in the List B pieces. Candidates are usually better at slowing down than getting faster, so it will be helpful to explain the concept of a balanced rubato during the practice period.

Dynamics tend to be more smoothly graded in the styles chosen for this list, and ability to mould the tone evenly in each hand is something to aim for at all stages. Subtlety of tone colour and control of rubato within the stylistic discipline of the pieces are high priorities. Often the pieces have descriptive titles, giving a clue to the mood and atmosphere of the music.

LIST C

This list offers something for everyone. There is tremendous variety – jazz pieces, contemporary items and a host of other styles – which should make it easy to find exactly the right choice for your pupils.

In the early grades the jazz items are always hugely popular. Candidates can manage quite difficult rhythms when they like the music. Strongly dynamic pieces, such as the all-time hit *Top Cat!* from the 2009 & 2010 Grade 3 syllabus, seem to capture the imagination of thousands of candidates throughout the world.

With such variety on offer, it's important to go to the heart of what each piece really requires to make an effective performance. Very often this means having a feel for the underlying beat, which will be more pro-nounced in the jazz pieces but still vital in many contemporary items. Colourful playing, evoking the various moods and sound worlds, will be enjoyable to explore, and candidates often feel they can relax and commu-nicate these pieces, achieving more of a sense of performance than they manage with pieces from either of the two other lists.

Swung rhythm is an issue right from Grade 1. This is not the place to give a detailed description (which really needs a demonstration to make the point), but it will help pupils to imagine that 4/4 time becomes 12/8, so that a dotted-quaver, semiquaver rhythm sounds more like crotchet, qua-ver. Pupils often catch on to this in certain parts of the piece, but find it difficult to be consistent, therefore causing the examiner to comment: 'Try to keep an even rhythm.' This does not mean that the swung rhythm has not been noticed, but usually indicates that there's an inconsistency in managing this throughout the performance. It is also perfectly acceptable to play the piece 'straight', especially in the lower grades, as long as the mood and relaxed feel of this style still come across. In the higher grades, the jazz pieces are quite sophisticated and often need a sense of swing and appreciation of whichever jazz style is appropriate to the piece.

In List C the metronome mark is often the composer's, so it pays to take notice and check carefully; as in Lists A and B, a metronome mark in square brackets indicates that it is an editorial suggestion, allowing a little more freedom of choice.

Young pupils often have a refreshingly open mind about contemporary items. Teachers may find some of the pieces slightly off-putting, but may be surprised to find that their students can get inside the music quite quickly and thoroughly enjoy playing in a different idiom.

Candidates are free to choose the order of their three pieces. It may well be wise to put the more technically demanding List A piece somewhere other than first in the exam. Many pupils start with their favourite piece, which helps their confidence when they come to tackle the others. It is sometimes rather disappointingly obvious why a piece has been left until last!

The extensive selection for each grade should ensure that each one of your candidates is happy and comfortable with the choice and order of his or her pieces. As teachers will be well aware, the candidate's attitude of mind as he or she enters the exam room is inevitably reflected in the result.

The lifespan of this new piano syllabus will mark a change at ABRSM, as I hand over the role of Chief Examiner to my successor John Holmes, as this book is published. With his new responsibilities, John hopes to provide a hub of communication and support for music teachers. If you have any queries arising from this publication, do not hesitate to contact him, preferably by email (chiefexaminer@abrsm.ac.uk).

We hope that these notes will inspire you, as you explore the piano syllabus repertoire.

Clara Taylor

GRADE 1

Pupils will usually have been learning for up to eighteen months by the time Grade 1 is on the horizon. They may have taken the Prep Test during this time, in which case they will probably feel quite confident when facing this first real exam. A wide choice of pieces should help to keep motivation high, so why not have some alternatives prepared, then choose the best three as the exam approaches? The criteria for assessment for all grades are printed in *These Music Exams* – a useful source of reference for teachers.

A:1 Anon. *Menuet in F*

Not many learners are as fortunate as Wolfgang and Nannerl Mozart, who each had a book of pieces compiled specifically for them. The gently flowing phrases and clear texture of this dance from Nannerl's volume evoke much of the elegance and grace of the eighteenth century.

Rhythmic patterns are mostly straightforward until the final bars in which the dotted figure and triplet may need extra care. In addition, the repeated crotchets in the first half must remain poised and the all-too-common fault of adding an extra beat at the double bar midway should be avoided.

Although the piece seems to consist mostly of two-bar units, thinking in longer phrases, especially through bars 5–8 and 13–16, will help to give more of a fluid shape and momentum. The detached crotchets should be clearly separated against the legato quavers, as recommended; however, adding some slurs to the left hand (e.g. in bar 15) might provide a stylish enhancement.

Mellow, gently shaped tone, with the dynamic level never becoming too robust, will suit the dance's overall character. Work on demonstrating an ability to balance the tune and accompaniment, and take care to stop stray thumb accents from spoiling the tapered phrase-endings. The diminuendo at bars 7–8 prepares the way for the *piano*, and a carefully paced ritardando will bring the piece to a graceful close.

A:2 Haydn *Andante*

Nowhere is Haydn's sense of humour more evident than in this symphonic movement with its *fortissimo* 'wake-up', surely one of the most famous

5

chords in all music. Although there are some changes of hand-position to negotiate, this arrangement fits well under the fingers, in addition to offering your pupil the opportunity to experience some genuinely witty music.

The semiquavers (bars 18, 19, 23) give the clue to the tempo, which must be measured and poised. Although each phrase has its own inherent shape, suspense can be created at the start by keeping the tone quiet and detaching the quavers lightly, as if on tip-toe. The cello section of the orchestra comes briefly to prominence as the left hand plays the melody at bar 9, and the 'surprise' *fortissimo* chord in bar 16, which needs all the strength of a full orchestra, can be as musically dramatic as possible.

The second half may need extra practice to ensure safe note-patterns and good hand co-ordination – the contrary-motion arpeggio figure in bars 21–2 is especially tricky. The pace must remain the same as before, with no hint of speeding up as the music becomes louder. Gently separated slurs, taking care not to accent the offbeat notes, together with clear, precise staccato, will add definition and style to the phrasing. The crescendo will have maximum impact if the *piano* at bar 17 is sufficiently quiet.

A:3 Hook *Gavotta*

Many players will be attracted to the athleticism of this piece with its energetic quaver movement and straightforward notes. The hand-position remains the same throughout and there are no difficult rhythms to negotiate.

Examiners often hear performances (especially of music with a strong natural momentum) that begin with great enthusiasm at a cracking pace, only to fall apart after a few bars! Although the notes might appear easy, there are a number of danger spots where co-ordination of the hands is liable to falter. Pupils must therefore develop the skill of setting a realistic, sustainable tempo.

A well-rounded hand-position will enable the fingers to articulate the quavers incisively at all dynamic levels, and with no overlap of the fingers – especially the notoriously lazy fourth and fifth! Independence is needed to distinguish between the detached repeated notes and smooth quavers at the start; practising slowly a five-finger exercise, alternating legato and staccato between the hands, may help to achieve this skill. If the suggested slurring in bars 13–15 seems unnecessarily complicated, the quavers may be played smoothly with phrasing interest being provided instead by a mixture of detached and slurred left-hand crotchets. The *piano* in bar 5 may be introduced by a diminuendo in the previous bar, whereas the echoes in the second half will be created by sharply defined dynamics and a slight separation of the phrases.

A:4 J. C. F. Bach *Schwaebisch in D*

This attractive rustic dance by one of J. S. Bach's composer-sons is a relatively straightforward choice with few awkward corners. The tempo, although unhurried, should be felt as one-in-a-bar, with the second and third quavers kept light, especially at the ends of phrases.

Right-hand notes should pose few problems, although care is needed to maintain fluency when the thumb shifts upwards in bars 4–5 and 12–13. Similarly, an extra beat must not be added at the double bar-line midway. A few tricky changes of hand-position in the bass part may need separate practice to ensure confident fingering.

A little phrasing is indicated, but choice is mainly left to the candidate. Slurring the first bar of each four-bar phrase will contrast well with the staccato that follows, and the two-note slurs marked in bars 4 and 11 imply lightly detached second and third beats.

The absence of dynamic markings gives the player free rein to explore his or her own ideas. A strong, confident start and finish would be effective, and dropping back to *piano* at bar 9 would allow a crescendo to be made towards the final phrase.

Careful pacing is needed to manage the ending convincingly. A gradual rallentando over the last two bars would be more appropriate than an 'emergency stop' at the final bar-line!

A:5 Naudot *Babiole*

The French word *babiole* translates to 'toy' or 'trifle', a title that seems to suit this playful piece. It holds few difficulties in the notes: the right hand is responsible for much of the activity, while the left remains largely within five-finger positions.

Despite the time signature of four-in-a-bar, thinking in minim beats will give airiness to the rhythm. Clarity of fingerwork (especially in the quavers) will be crucial to ensure a truly stable pulse, and pupils should take care not to rush the longer notes at the ends of phrases. The recurring two-quaver/crotchet figure that opens three of the piece's four phrases may be slurred, dropping the right hand and wrist on to the accents and lifting off gently at the third note of the group. Elsewhere, detaching the crotchets while sustaining the minims is a stylish option, and in those bars where the two are combined good independence of the hands will be needed.

Although much of the piece is marked *forte*, starting each phrase slightly quieter than marked gives scope for a crescendo towards the midway point. The opportunity to play really quietly in bars 5–8 should not be missed, and the final bars need decisive tone and rhythmic poise to round off the piece with real confidence.

A:6 Purcell *A Song Tune*

This elegant piece, best suited to pupils with a large left-hand stretch, needs a smooth, well-shaped tone and a two-in-a-bar flow to convey its song-like character – remember that it is not a march!

The most challenging aspect is likely to be the sustaining of notes within the left hand's two-part texture. Initially, dividing the two 'voices' between the hands will enable the suspensions to be heard clearly. A perfect legato can't always be achieved when the left hand plays both voices, but, wherever possible, the parts should be held for their full value without any overlap of sound. In bar 6 the (middle C) thumb note must be sustained while the fifth finger moves from C to F. Fingering the following quavers with 3-1-2-1 may be best for a small hand and, if an octave stretch is not possible, the dotted minim in bar 7 may be released early.

The piece falls into two phrases of equal length. Singing the right-hand melody at a suitable pitch is the best way to feel the shape and span of the musical line. Each phrase has a natural rise and fall of tone; however, the Scotch snap recommended in bar 8 seems to call for a strong, proud ending.

Finally, don't be put off by the ornaments (marked or suggested). At this grade it is best to modify or even omit them if they prove problematic.

B:1 Pauline Hall *Tarantella*

Whether dancing to cure a tarantula's bite or not, the performance must convey a sense of frenzy and excitement. Rhythmic drive, energy and clearly articulated quavers are the order of the day. This shouldn't be too problematic as the music lies neatly in a five-finger position throughout – other than at the end, when the left hand needs to cross swiftly over the right with a flamboyant finish.

Attentive use of the accents will help to underpin the rhythmic thrust and, particularly in bars 13–14, will aid the hand synchronization. The intended quaver speed needs to be considered when embarking on the opening dotted crotchets, in order to reduce the possibility of fluctuation in the pulse. The piece requires much dynamic variety: the opening two bars should launch the performance with each dotted crotchet gaining in intensity – practise finding the right note pressure to ensure the opening is not too tentative.

The co-ordination and balance of the left hand's chords will need some care. Students might experiment by playing first the bottom note, then adding the 5th and then the 3rd/4th – listening to the balance with the right hand at each stage. When the full triad is played, the C and D act as a pivot between the chords.

This piece is a winner, and provided that a tight rein is kept on the pulse a confident performance should ensue.

B:2 Martha Mier *A Story from Long Ago*

Imagine a cowboy playing this soulful ballad on his harmonica around a campfire, and the scene will be set. An unhurried pace will allow each note of the beautiful and idiomatic melody to receive a warm, cantabile touch.

Singing the melody through is the best way to develop a natural sense of phrasing. Although a student might feel a little self-conscious at first, it really is worth the effort to persevere in this. Try singing the melody in stages, beginning with the two-bar phrases (as in bars 1–2 and 3–4) and then, with greater reserves of breath, the following four-bar phrase (bars 5–8). On the piano the tone must be firm throughout, especially when the tune is in the left hand; the sound should be kept particularly energized in the final *piano* phrase (bars 17–18).

Pedalling might be too advanced for some at this stage or not physically possible for others, and (as indicated in the footnotes) it is optional in the exam. However, if pedal can be employed where marked it will increase the tonal resonance and fluency. For the straightforward legato pedalling that is required, the student should ensure that the depression of the pedal is delayed until just after the first beat of the bar is played in order to avoid smudging the melodic line. As always, encourage 'pedalling with the ears'.

B:3 Swinstead *A Tender Flower*

Not necessarily green but certainly supple and sensitive fingers will be needed here. A charming and comforting piece to play, it has few technical or rhythmic challenges, allowing the pianist to concentrate on the musical and tonal features: good legato and an expressive sense of phrasing.

Even at this stage a cantabile tone should be encouraged. The touch must not be tentative, and the left hand's drones need to support and sustain the melody in the right without overpowering it. In the right hand, the shift of hand-position between bars 1 and 2 (and bars 5 and 6) will require repetition practice, both to safely prepare the new triad position and to play the quavers rhythmically. The right-hand jump back to G in bar 3 will also need careful preparation.

As the title suggests, the piece needs to be played with tenderness and affection. Breathing with and possibly singing the phrases will help to develop a sense of shape and line. The student will really enjoy the natural arch of the phrase (bars 3 and 4), and should pay careful attention to the last note dying away and blending into the G of bar 5. In bars 7 and 8 the left hand shares the expressive features, but the crescendo and decrescendo must be carefully graded. Thinking of a cello or bassoon playing this line might help to provide the appropriate tone colour.

The piece concludes with a carefully paced rallentando. After the final semibreve is counted precisely, the hands should be lifted off gently so as not to disturb the lovely atmosphere that has been created.

B:4 Rybicki *Longing*

This poignant piece is full of subtlety and would suit the more sensitive student. It presents good opportunities for playing expressively, and for cultivating a legato touch and cantabile tone.

The slurs have been carefully drawn and require some thought. To begin, the left hand is grouped in six and then in three crotchets: while it is important to make this differentiation, make only a gentle break at the end of each slur to avoid disturbing the rhythmic flow and musical line. Treat the right hand's paired slurs (last quaver of the bar to the dotted minim) like little sighs, using a coaxing touch but without any sense of rushing or over-accenting. Continue these stylistic nuances as the piece develops.

A wide range of expressive colour will be expected, especially from the crescendo marked in bar 9, which should begin softly. *Forte* is reached at the climax in bar 13 before subsiding to the *piano* of the opening. The crescendo's intensity is motivated by the left-hand crotchet movement, and a good cantabile should be achievable with forearm weight projected into the right hand's sweeping octave leaps. The syncopated rhythms in bar 14 should not pose a problem if the quaver movement is kept in mind. A carefully paced rallentando brings this haunting piece to its conclusion; a very gentle lift of the hands on the final rest will prevent the atmosphere from being broken too soon.

B:5 Schubert *The Trout*

What a fine introduction to the songs of Schubert this is! Christian Friedrich Daniel Schubart wrote the poem *Die Forelle* ('The Trout'), which Schubert set; becoming familiar with the poem will bring enjoyment of the story as well as the music. After mastering the notes, listening to the song (and the piano quintet based on the song) may inspire and also lead the student to an interpretation with a definite sense of fun.

In the opening four-bar phrase (and the second phrase), particular attention needs to be paid to the paired slurs. The player should guard against any tendency to clip or over-accent them; a gentle detached lift on the second crotchet will prevent any disturbance to the line. The second part of the phrase requires more legato and expressive shaping, and the rest that concludes the phrase should be treated like a singer's breath. From bars 9 to 16 a warm legato cello tone is needed in the left hand; think in long shapely lines here.

Once the melody is fluent and flows between the hands, give attention to the balance of the chords. The left hand at bars 3, 7 and 17 will require reasonable weight to sustain the semibreve, but, again, avoid over-accenting the notes. The right hand in bars 9–16 requires only a lightly supportive touch.

B:6 Schumann *Soldatenmarsch (Soldiers' March)*

Perhaps not as straightforward as it might appear, this cheerful piece requires crisp dotted rhythms, precisely measured quavers (notes and rests) and a firm touch. This is a march with a definite 'spring in the step'.

There might be a tendency to rush the dotted rhythms so some initial tapping of these rhythms against semiquavers would be beneficial. The quaver followed by a quaver rest must be accurately counted, thus ensuring that the quaver is not too clipped. Some clapping and marching in time will also help to promote the stress as being on the first and not the second beat.

The piece lies under the hands quite well, but secure and consistent fingering will be needed, especially at bars 3–4, 7–8 and 23–4. No dynamic variation is marked but where *forte* is absent a lesser dynamic may be implied. The dotted rhythms should always be strong, but the quaver chords could be slightly lighter (especially at bars 19–20 and 23–4) and a warmer, smoother tone is necessary at bars 17–18 and 21–2.

Balancing or 'voicing' the chords throughout needs some consideration. The 'soprano' melody must sing out over the homophonic texture beneath; sustaining this while lightly detaching the rest of the chord will provide an effective practice method as well as promoting aural alertness. With this aspect mastered, the piece will have an added sparkle and polish.

C:1 S. C. Foster *Camptown Races*

This cheerful arrangement allows your pupils to enjoy one of Stephen Foster's most popular songs as a piano solo. Learners must not be put off by the multitude of flats in the key signature; the piece is pentatonic, played entirely on the black notes, and can easily be learned by rote.

A staccato touch, from the tip of a well-curved finger, is needed for much of the piece. Where staccato in one hand is contrasted with legato in the other (as in bar 2), the required co-ordination and sensation of hand independence can be practised outside the context of the piece using any notes, perhaps of your pupil's own choice. One way of tackling the co-ordination required in bars 9 and 11 is to play equal quavers in the left hand, carefully aligning those in the right with the second and fourth. Once this placement has become habitual, the left-hand dotted rhythm can be reintroduced.

The arranger has asked for a dynamic palette of mostly *mezzo-forte* and *forte*, so sturdy fingers and a firm attack are called for. A strong, clear sound allied with a steady tempo (crotchet = *c*.96 works well) and a constant, stable pulse should give the music its sprightly character.

Finding all the G♭s on the piano will be useful preparation for learning the last three bars. Have fun!

C:2 Fiona Macardle *Late at Night*

This music suggests a domestic scene: the last family member still up lolls comfortably in an easy chair in front of the telly or fireplace, entering a dozy haze as the music ends. The performance direction is 'sleepy', and crotchet = *c*.96 provides a relaxed pace but one that holds the piece together musically, allowing a one-in-a-bar feeling and a soothing waltz-like lilt.

The composer gives four different dynamic levels; these should be audibly differentiated in performance. Dynamic gradations can be gauged outside the setting of the piece and incorporated into scale practice. You can ask for a scale to be played *mezzo-forte* or, conversely, your pupil can choose a dynamic level and ask you to guess which he or she has chosen. However, as this music is in the nature of a lullaby, the *mezzo-forte* should not be too enthusiastic. From bar 13 to the end, the *una corda* pedal can be applied.

Use of the sustaining pedal in the last two bars adds an appropriate woolliness to the sound and usefully introduces direct pedalling. For the well co-ordinated player, basic legato pedalling throughout, on a mainly bar-by-bar basis, is an option.

If the examiner is asleep at the end of this piece, you can be sure that the performance has been a great success!

C:3 Kevin Wooding *Vampire Blues*

Power rather than speed is essential for this humorous musical portrait. The pulse, at crotchet = *c*.126, must be rock-steady throughout so that even (as opposed to swung) quavers can be accurately realized. The composer highlights the need to count the rests carefully and, to this end, it is useful to clap the notated rhythms while the beat is tapped out with the foot – your pupil's, yours or both! When back at the keyboard, it is still useful to check how placement of the notes relates to a clapped beat, thus further promoting rhythmic precision.

Suggested fingerings are helpful but an alternative to those shown in bars 1 and 3 is to start with the right hand on finger 4 and to use 3 instead of 1 in the left hand, thence keeping both hands in a single position. This may benefit larger hands in particular. There is also another option for the right hand in bars 9 and 11 which is to use 2-3-5-4 for the first four notes, again minimizing thumb usage.

The dynamic indications are either *mezzo-forte* or *forte*, so strength of tone is needed. Use the weight of a freely dropping forearm but ensure that *mezzo-forte* is given noticeably less force than *forte*. Hand and foot can descend in mutual attack for the 'bite' at the end – but don't worry too much; this vampire sounds pretty harmless to me!

C:4 Bartók *Quasi adagio*

This rather mournful little number is likely to appeal to the more introverted pianist. One can imagine a simple story of disappointment being gently narrated, perhaps by an older to a younger person.

Since there is no need for the right hand to move outside a five-finger position, it seems expedient not to disturb this. For example, in bars 7–8 and 17–18 the slurred effect can be achieved equally well using fingering 3-3-2-2-1-1. The left-hand part is similar throughout, but the changes of position during bars 16–18 will need to be planned carefully. One practising technique would be to repeat rhythmically a five-note cluster (A to E) in the right hand while focusing attention on the keyboard positions involved in the left hand – which needs to be held forwards if the F♯ is to be reached easily.

The loudest dynamic marking is *piano*, so hand and finger movements need to be contained, with the right-hand fifth finger rising just enough for the upper E to re-sound. However, the hairpins suggest a dynamic rise and fall. To practise this, try physically leaning forwards then backwards so that the sound seems to loom up from the piano. The *una corda* pedal can be applied at the end.

The inquisitive learner might like to know that much of this piece uses the Dorian mode (from A).

C:5 Janina Garścia *Allegretto*

Eastern European composers have a distinguished track record in writing attractive educational music, and this miniature sonatina movement is no exception. For the more advanced learner it is also a very good introduction to the pentatonic scale (C major pentatonic, in this case).

A crisp staccato attack is needed for all the quavers. To achieve this, strike the key then pull the finger rapidly upwards and inwards in a curved but contained trajectory. An alternative to the printed note distribution is to open the piece using the fourth finger on G and second on E, then to play all the notes in bar 3 with the right hand rather than taking the E with the left. Also, for the sake of consistency, the left-hand part in bars 9–10 and 13–14 can helpfully be fingered 5-4-2-1-2-1.

A tempo of crotchet = *c*.108 yields a suitable *allegretto* pace. Since a steady pulse is important, some practice with a metronome may be advisable, although a very slight concluding ritenuto could be effective.

Hands can be held very close to the keyboard to achieve *pianissimo*, but rather higher for the *forte* passages. In the former, use of the *una corda* pedal will add to the effect.

This is certainly a good piece for developing a vivid sense of dynamic opposition.

C:6 Lajos Papp *Grasshopper*

This descriptive little character piece could be imaginatively linked to a grasshopper story ('A Day in the Life of'), but it is also a splendid introduction to staccato playing.

The two hands do not actually play together, so the piece presents no serious co-ordination problems. For much of the piece the left hand uses the same notes, so it might be a good idea to memorize these early on in the learning process.

The right-hand part may take a little longer to master and it would be worth practising consecutive triads, outside the context of the piece, starting on three white notes before introducing a black note into the middle, played by finger 3. Most of the staccato playing involves chords, so a confident wrist-and-finger staccato technique is called for. Fingers need to be curved with tips alert and ready to pull rapidly upwards from the keyboard after striking. There also needs to be a 'spring' in the wrist, which should remain relaxed but not too loose or the tone is likely to become flabby.

Sound levels are generally strong (mostly *mezzo-forte* to *forte*), so the downward attack into the keyboard can be deliberate without being unduly harsh. However, some subtlety is required if the hairpins are to be observed. A tempo of minim = *c.*72 will work well.

Enjoy the story!

GRADE 2

Lessons will have been learnt from Grade 1, and pupils will probably want to play something similar to their favourite piece from the last exam. The pacing of the preparation, not forgetting the supporting tests, will probably be easier with the experience of Grade 1 safely in the past.

A:1 Daquin *Suite de la réjouissance*

To portray the exuberant and stately mood of this gavotte, one could imagine as the setting for this dance the Palace of Versailles, in all its Baroque grandeur.

The tempo indication makes the quavers manageable and enables the elegant dance character to emerge. With neat fingerwork and precisely placed octaves the piece does not present many technical or rhythmic challenges.

The uplifting musical spirit must be conveyed, but the examiner will also look for an awareness of Baroque conventions, especially in awarding those distinction marks. Therefore the touch should be light yet firm. Articulation and dynamics are not included and will need to be carefully planned. For example, a shapely and articulate melody line over lightly detached quavers in the left hand will help establish a confident sense of style. Encourage pupils to experiment with different ideas, however consistency and simplicity will be the best guidelines.

Dynamic contrast would certainly add interest. In order to achieve different colours try to think of the dynamics as orchestral textures. For example, the opening might be trumpet and strings (*forte*), bars 9–16 strings alone (*piano*), and the middle (bars 17–28) oboes and bassoons (starting *piano* and beginning a crescendo from bar 21).

The cadential embellishments do not pose too many problems but should be given careful attention so that the result will add stylistic appeal. Finally, playing the da capo will be necessary to give the music structure and balance.

A:2 Pauline Hall, based on Haydn *Military Minuet*

Listening to Haydn's 'Military' Symphony (ideally with a score in hand) would be a good starting-point to get a sense of the music's pomp and splendour. The dance character needs to be underpinned by a tempo and pulse of military precision. The suggested metronome marking of crotchet = *c.*120 gives an appropriate spring in the step.

The semiquaver anacrusis provides each phrase with a suitable lift and must gracefully and lightly flow into the first beat of the bar that follows (with care taken not to over-accent the second beat): perhaps imagine a bow or curtsy here. However, for the music to maintain its momentum and avoid becoming staid it will be necessary to think in four-bar phrases. The orchestral performance will give some idea of tonal nuance.

In this arrangement the student must create a clear change in colour between bars 1–8 and 9–16: wind and possibly percussion are suggested by the first section, but bars 9–16, the middle section, require a lighter, more lyrical approach. And the da capo (which will be expected in the exam) could be full orchestra.

There are two possible scenarios for the ending: it could either be loud and in tempo, or have a more tapered and sedate finish with a *poco rall.* and a slight decrescendo.

A:3 Krieger *Bourrée*

This Baroque dance is better thought of in duple rather than quadruple metre, as it will give a suitably sprightly character and will help overcome a tendency to emphasize the third beat. Clear part-playing and consistent articulation are the essential elements behind a successful performance.

In bars 1–4 and 9–12 the crotchets could be lightly detached but the phrasing in bars 5–8 should be either completely legato or with crotchets played three-quarters of their length (dotted quaver). The right- and left-hand parts may be thought of as a duet, for which the student could suggest two different instruments or voices, or, better, play or sing the parts separately to help get a sense of shape and phrasing.

Although not necessarily in accordance with Baroque keyboard practice, employing some dynamic contrast will work well in a piano performance of this work. A light yet bright touch would suit bars 1–4 and 9–12, whereas a gentler tone quality is more appropriate in bars 5–8. In the exam the first repeat should be played, as this will give the performance balance. The repeat of these first four bars could be an echo to provide a contrasted tone colour.

The ornaments (as with the other directions) are editorial markings but the little embellishments at the cadence points add sparkle and stylistic refinement – and will certainly impress the examiner if executed in a clear and elegant manner.

A:4 Hummel *Dialogue Taquin*

This flowing conversational piece should also have a playful, teasing character, as implied in the title.

The fingering will require some careful planning initially, but in general it does not pose too many technical challenges. However, some gentle rotation facility will be needed in the right hand at bars 11–12. The quavers here should be played with a legato touch, although for variety the left-hand crotchets in these bars could be lightly detached. A gently swung cantabile will be necessary on the accented minims in order to sustain them above the quaver movement; here it is almost as if the hands are trying to talk over each other. Teacher and pupil could perhaps sing the individual lines as a duet to get a sense of the dialogue.

If gracefully tapered, the cadences at bars 8 and 16 will give a real sense of the elegant style. The student must listen carefully to the sound of the minim dying away and then match and blend the tone to the following crotchet. This is easier said than done and should first be tried in slow motion, perhaps in single notes to begin with. The rests throughout the piece require absolute precision, especially when the minim needs to be heard on its own. No dynamics are marked in the first eight bars but *mezzo-forte* would encourage a singing tone quality.

A:5 Petzold *Menuet [II] in G minor*

This dignified and somewhat plaintive dance lends itself to a stately, unhurried tempo. Good blending between the hands is essential. Overall the piece requires an even, legato touch. The second and third beats in bars 2 and 10, however, should be lightly detached; this could be employed elsewhere in both hands, at bars 15, 23 and 31 (second and third beats). A more varied approach to phrasing is possible, but aiming for simplicity is generally best.

The ornamentation is not too demanding and, if musically incorporated, will add stylish appeal (not to mention distinction marks). The mordent in bars 8 and 15 should be executed like a trill beginning on the upper note, but use a straightforward mordent in bars 9 and 22. Ornaments can be simplified or even omitted, however, if they prove problematic.

Although not marked, some dynamic contrast would add interest and provide shape and structure. Various options would lead to a musically pleasing result but, again, simplicity is effective. A slight easing of tempo and tone in bar 24 (second and third beats) will give poise; thereafter the dynamic level can be restored gradually to its opening level.

Provided systematic fingering is used there are few technical challenges, but bar 27 will need careful practice. Slightly emphasize the G-F#-G, and encourage a gently rotating motion when the left hand's notes are lightly added.

A:6 Vaughan Williams *Two-Part Invention in G*

This charming piece is a good introduction to part playing, encouraging independence of the hands (though it is certainly less demanding than the Inventions of J. S. Bach). Practising hands separately will be required to develop a legato line. Fingering must be carefully planned and systematic, with special care taken not to over-accent the left-hand thumb on the second beat in bars 7, 17 and 27. Imagining two singing voices or two contrasting instruments should encourage a beautiful and seamless blend between the hands. The examiner will be looking for a gently flowing motion throughout the piece.

As the piece unfolds it will be easy for the student to feel the natural contours of the phrase, and the expression marks highlight this. Since the dynamic markings are extremely subtle (*piano* down to *pianississimo*), begin practice by playing at a *mezzo-piano* to *mezzo-forte* level, until confidence has been gained and a sweet singing tone secured. Even in performance a firm rather than tentative touch should be aimed for, especially as the piano used in the exam will probably be unfamiliar.

The piece works well without the repeat, which will not be expected in the exam. The *poco rit.* provides a nicely poised ending and leads this meandering little piece to a natural conclusion.

B:1 Berkovich *Mazurka*

A strong sense of pulse, together with clear phrasing and accentuation, lies at the heart of a good performance of this attractive piece. The mood is upbeat and joyous, perhaps conjuring up a rustic scene of a lively folk dance.

The note patterns of the outer sections generally fall easily under the fingers, although care is needed to ensure that both right-hand chord notes sound together. Co-ordinating the phrasing detail between the hands, which will require slow practice, is one of the main challenges here. Short 'snappy' semiquavers, each of which can be slurred to the following note, and clear second-beat accents will help to give poise and character to the rhythm – there must be no hint of rushing at the crescendos. Your pupil will probably have already encountered slurs from a strong to a weaker beat; here, however, the stress is reversed to give prominence to the second (main beat) note. The left-hand slurs, which suggest a drone accompaniment, may be lightly detached at the end of each bar to 'let in the air'.

The mood becomes more forceful in bar 9 as the tonality briefly reaches D minor. The rhythm is more complex here, especially the upbeat quavers (which should not be mistaken for semiquavers), and the leaps in the right hand may need extra care.

B:2 Brahms *The Sandman*

One can picture the Schumann children standing around the piano singing this delightful song, which was specially arranged for them by Uncle Johannes! Sensitive players who can produce a good singing tone will be attracted to this simple yet effective arrangement.

The largely three-part texture should be played as smoothly as possible. Practice will be needed to sustain the bass G in bar 1 while releasing the 'tenor' notes cleanly. Elsewhere, however, it may not always be possible to hold both chord notes for their full value – for instance, the left-hand D in bar 3 must be released in order to be repeated while the F♯ is joined to the following note.

Although the piece falls into four main phrases, there are further subdivisions during each line. Singing the melody, breathing at phrase-endings, is the best guide to shaping and sustaining the musical line. Although some pupils may be reluctant singers, most can be encouraged to sing at a comfortable pitch, with a little support and reassurance. A leisurely yet flowing tempo will allow the phrases to move smoothly and easily, with no unwanted accents. The climax, albeit a gentle one, occurs on the third line, but elsewhere the *piano* dynamic needs good key-control to ensure that all notes of the chord blend. Although not indicated, a diminuendo and slight ritardando in the final bars will suit the sleepy mood of the ending.

B:3 Schubert *Trio*

Suitable for a confident pupil with a good sense of keyboard geography, this arrangement captures much of the Viennese charm and lilt of this delightful symphonic movement. Although written for orchestra, the shapely character of this melody reminds us of Schubert's fame as a writer of songs (more than 600 of them).

A well-shaped cantabile tone and clearly defined phrasing will breathe life into the melodic lines, which are played chiefly by the right hand. Each phrase has its own natural rise and fall, and careful balancing of the hands will ensure that the tune always sings. The changes of hand position in the accompaniment at the opening and closing eight bars may need separate practice, with care taken to show clearly the contrast between short and long phrases. Carefully paced crotchets throughout and light offbeat notes will help to create that all-important two-in-a-bar lilt.

The *forte* in bar 8, which comes as a surprise, briefly disturbs the placid mood of the opening. Each dynamic level in these four bars needs clarity, with the right-hand phrases separated; this will lead on effectively to a moment of repose, if the ritardando and diminuendo are well paced.

A firm tone in the left hand will enable the 'cello' section of the orchestra to assume prominence briefly at the upbeat into bar 13 (a tempo), before the interest switches back to the right hand for the final four bars.

B:4 Duvernoy *Andantino*

The word 'Andantino' may not conjure up much atmosphere around this lovely piece, with its easy-flowing melody above a gently rocking accompaniment, so another title might be created for it – 'Strolling in the Countryside' or 'Daydreaming', for instance. You can explain to your pupil the ternary (A–B–A) structure, perhaps also exploring the concept of modulation as the music moves to the dominant key of E major in bars 13–16.

Practising the left-hand quavers separately, keeping fingers close to the keys and ensuring that the repeated thumb notes are really subdued, is the first step to achieving that all-important balance of tone between the hands. At the start the right-hand melody should sing gently and smoothly above the accompaniment, rising and falling in tone in accordance with the melodic contours. To maintain a legato feel, take care in bars 11–12 where the hands reverse roles: keep the right hand light and let the left hand sing out a little. A flexible rhythmic approach, moving forward slightly towards the peaks of phrases and then easing off, will allow the music to breathe.

The mood becomes a little more robust at bar 9 and the dynamic contrasts should be clearly shown. Slight separation of the right hand's one-bar phrases will enhance the echo effects. Care should be taken not to hurry in the louder phrases and the right hand must lift efficiently to ensure clarity in the quavers. A slight ritardando in bar 16 will ease the transition back to *piano* for the da capo (which must be played).

B:5 Gurlitt *Gavotte in A minor*

The teasing yet graceful character of this delightful nineteenth-century 'take' on an earlier musical form should prove a real winner with musical candidates who have good finger-facility. The notes fit comfortably under the fingers, and the piece has the added advantage of identical patterns in the first and last sections.

The light, airy character of the opening section can be achieved by feeling two beats in a bar, rather than the stated four. Highlight the characteristic gavotte rhythm, with its middle-of-the-bar starts of phrase, by making a slight crescendo towards the first beat and gently tapering the phrase-endings. Although the right-hand figuration suggests units of one or two bars, thinking in longer four-bar phrases will help to give flow and impetus to the music. Detaching the left hand's unslurred crotchets will enhance the rhythmic buoyancy. The right-hand quavers need clarity and definition within the gentle dynamic, and bars 2–3 and 6–7 might need separate practice to ensure that fingerings are securely learnt.

The mood becomes more dramatic and insistent at bar 9 as the crescendo and left-hand accents lead to the *forte* climax. Neat co-ordination between the hands is important here, with contrasts between legato and staccato clearly defined, and care should be taken not to rush the rests. A slight ritardando at the beginning of bar 16 will help to prepare the return to the opening mood.

B:6 Tchaikovsky *Waltz*

Nobody wrote finer melodies than Tchaikovsky and here is one of his best! In this effective arrangement of the famous *Sleeping Beauty* waltz, melodic interest is shared between the hands, thereby posing a good musical challenge.

Imagining the graceful movements of the corps de ballet will provide inspiration for the smooth cantabile tone needed to sustain the long melodic phrases. Much of the piece moves gently in one-in-a-bar until the hemiola (from bar 25) produces the effect of a slower pulse, despite no actual change to the basic crotchet speed. Bars 15–17 and 23–5 are potential hazard-zones worth singling out for separate practice, as are the left hand's chords in the final section.

The ability to produce different levels of tone between the hands is crucial throughout the piece. Although the dynamic temperature doesn't rise high in the first half, gentle inflections of tone will breathe life into the phrasing. Careful listening will ensure that the right hand accompanies, rather than overpowers, the melody in the left hand. The ascending scale in bars 7–8 assumes momentary prominence, but the right hand's real turn for the limelight occurs at bar 16. At this point the roles are reversed until the end of the piece. Beginning the crescendo towards the final left-hand accents will be more effective if started more quietly than *mezzo-forte*.

C:1 John Kember *Bah-ba-doo bah*

You may wonder if the composer has had a strange turn, given the unusual title of this cool little number. It is in fact the 'scat' equivalent of the right hand's opening motif – so if the suggested swung rhythm isn't enough to give the feel here, the title certainly will.

Put embarrassment to one side and encourage students not just to sing the first line 'scat' style but to put the whole piece to 'vocables' – effectively made-up sounds imitating a soloing instrument. It will then become obvious how to interpret the notated articulation detail, which is simply a brave attempt to show the phrasing and emphasis that would come naturally to a jazz musician. It is worth remembering that the rests are just as important as the notes in creating the right character.

The left hand is the rhythm section and falls nicely under the fingers. A little 'push' on the second and fourth beats will give this the appropriate momentum and energy, as will a 'semi-staccato' feel, which is more a shuffling of the feet than skipping. Suitable dynamic contrast and shading exactly as marked will add the extra musical dimension and interest. Finally, don't forget the da capo, which gives the feel of the 'head, improvisation, return to the head' structure typical of jazz.

C:2 Timothy Salter *Cat being bold at first*

Anyone who has a cat will relish this descriptive piece and the images it conveys. Even the atonal idiom is appropriate, especially when you think of how far removed from a major or minor key the night-time cry of a cat can be. The suggested tempo works perfectly; after which it is counting, familiarity with the notes, and observation of the expressive detail that will dictate the performance's effectiveness.

Since the piece looks complex, writing in the letter names of the notes on leger lines will help with reading the notation. Learning much of it from memory is advisable, as any subservience to the music may well lead to hesitation under exam conditions. Memorizing can easily be done while focusing on exactly the right touch and sound; simply work in small sections, moving the music to one side once the patterns of that bar have become familiar. This will also encourage counting, listening and using the imagination well beyond anything that would be achievable when following the score.

The cat's increasing nervousness will only come across if the dynamics and articulation are boldly conveyed. The ritardando needs to be carefully controlled, and rests throughout must be held for their full length. There may be no notes written in the final bar, but hands, like the cat's paws, should stay still above the keys for the full, four, slowing beats.

C:3 Trad. American *Down by the Riverside*

The spacious and simple look of this optimistic spiritual, as well as the familiarity of its well-known tune, will attract students – and it is undoubtedly a very effective arrangement. It will rely on an unfaltering sense of pulse to avoid any initial unsteadiness, and also on a sensitivity to touch and articulation which will give the piece its rhythmic energy and gospel feel.

The opening left-hand crotchets should be almost full-length, the rests clearly defined and consecutive crotchets only just detached. Syncopated rhythms and staccato crotchets in the right hand will work very well if played precisely and neatly just as marked. The melodic line responds to a somewhat understated approach, although it does require vocal shape and a confident 'work-song' tone in order to sing above the accompaniment.

The later right-hand chords will need preparation in advance, with the hands moving ahead of the beat, but the naturally detached nature of the music will help this. All chords should be lifted together and carefully balanced towards the top: resist the temptation in bars 21 and 23 to lift the left hand's minims in sympathy with the right hand.

The sparsity of expressive markings gives even more scope for an imaginative use of dynamics and shading. These should be explored to add vocal interest; singing the song may give inspiration here, and pupils can pencil-in their ideas for personalizing the performance.

C:4 Elias Davidsson *Men's Dance*

This masculine dance conjures up the image of heavy boots and a sense of robust fun. It is full of musical depiction: the bold dynamic conveys hearty footsteps, offbeat rhythms imply awkward movements and the low register of the melody (after the double bar) suggests a macho chorus. Although the piece works fairly well at minim = 80 it is better slightly faster (but allow for the *più mosso*).

Co-ordination will be the main problem; the left-hand offbeat 5ths are not predictably placed yet they need a secure rhythmic identity. Work at the melody independently wherever it occurs, complete with phrasing and musical shading. Once secure, practise the chords: aim for a light, short sound – effectively a 'spring' of the hand from the bottom of the key, returning to the key surface for the next. Only then should the hands be put slowly together. As confidence grows, add more emphasis to the articulation and dynamics, and focus on the physical relationship between the hand movements.

Dynamic variation and shape will enhance the character: after the *mezzo-forte* in bar 9, explore the use of hairpins to shape the phrases in the middle section and create contrast between bars 9–14 and 17–22, but remember to save something for the *fortissimo* in bar 25. While these dancers seem rhythmically challenged, don't join them by shortening the semibreve in bar 33! It must have all four beats to 'show off' the final chord, as the dancers throw themselves into an exhausted heap on the floor.

C:5 Janina Garścia *In the Train*

This gently chugging piece is more an unhurried journey through the countryside than an intercity dash, though a tempo of crotchet = 140 is perhaps as slow as you will need to travel.

The left-hand part requires a light, steady staccato touch from the key's surface, with the smallest bounce at the wrist and a little weight behind the first note of each bar to convey energy and momentum; this will keep the train purposeful throughout. The subtle ritardandos later, however, need to be carefully judged to help ease the way around the bends, and the sudden drama of the *forte* in bar 9 should be conveyed with confidence.

The right hand is altogether different, a relaxing 'stretch' in the carriage, highlighted by the smooth line of the chords. It is important that the fingers are nicely legato at the top, the notes carefully overlapped with dynamic shading to the top of the phrase.

Bar 16 needs a sudden change of colour: staccato and a brighter tone at the top of the chords with a slightly grumpy accent in bar 17 (a passenger irritated at being woken?). In the right hand's chord in bar 31 a fingering of 3/1 would work better than 2/1. Finally, the right foot must be ready with the pedal for the last note, the train slowing for the final hiss of steam.

C:6 Christopher Norton *Cloudy Day*

This wonderfully evocative piece offers scope for colourful, musical playing. Imagine raindrops, falling slowly from a cloud-dark sky, the breeze building to a mournful sigh through the trees. Lighter clouds appear, unhurriedly part, and the gentle sun shines, warming the surroundings.

The opening left-hand chord should be gently and dryly placed, like the arid ground it depicts, while the right hand's raindrops fall steadily with a delicate, short staccato achieved from the surface of the keys and which dynamically follows the pitch contours. After a tiny comma (end of bar 4) the music is repeated more insistently and then the breeze arrives. Pedal can work from the very beginning of bar 9, with changes after the chords in bars 11 and 13, to blend the harmonies and hold the atmosphere as the right hand becomes increasingly dramatic. Maintain the *forte* until the sound dies down below the overall resonance of the pedalled sound-world in bar 16.

The calmer tone from bar 17 requires a sensitivity of touch in order to blend and avoid a dissonant mass of sound. This section should finish with the most poised of ritardandos before a clear breath of stillness over bars 20–21. You may encourage your pupil to explore the use of a sensitive rubato in bars 21–4, moving towards the top of the phrase and relaxing away into the beautiful shifting harmonies of the last bars – which should be enhanced by slow changes of pedal, blending the major chords.

GRADE 3

Perhaps it is time to be a little more adventurous in the choice of pieces, now that exams are more of a familiar experience. Something of quite a different style might broaden the pupil's outlook, so do explore the alternative pieces as well as the printed selection.

A:1 J. S. Bach *Prelude in C*

This impressive prelude could provide a dramatic opening to a Grade 3 recital. Improvisatory and organistic by nature, it begins with a wonderful C octave; this clearly suggests a rich 16′ stop on the pedal, with the swell box gently opening through the first few bars to provide the effective crescendo (editorial) in the right hand.

To promote the stately feel the right-hand and left-hand quavers should be kept legato throughout, but always with musical shape. The chords in the right hand need to be positive and grand, with a distinct start and end to show the rest clearly. The right-hand chord at the end of bar 6 should be neatly separated with the left hand to provide a lighter upbeat.

Bars 9–11, given their co-ordination challenges, are perhaps the most technically difficult bars of the piece. The lower mordent in the left hand may readily be missed out for initial practice – and indeed altogether if it proves too cumbersome. However, for an accomplished performance it will be best if the ornament is tucked in on the beat and the arm kept light with fingers allowed to move unimpeded by arm weight. The crotchets are best detached here. A crescendo from bar 9 would be wholly appropriate, as would dynamic shape to the quavers in bars 12 and 13.

Bar 14 presents musical and technical challenges: the semiquavers shouldn't arrive like an express train but should ease their way in with some improvisatory flexibility as the music moves purposefully towards the bold final cadence.

A:2 Dittersdorf *Englischer Tanz in A*

Thinking of morris dancing or the less exuberant barn dances, during the time of the first two King Georges, will help in understanding the polite and sophisticated, yet slightly light-hearted, nature of this English dance. It is less for the peasants than for the aristocracy and should therefore avoid being too heavy, fast or forceful.

Control, articulation and balance will be the crucial factors in conveying the dance character. The opening needs a lightness in the left hand and a bright, animated right-hand tone. The opening left-hand 3rds should be lightly staccato – as should the first two quavers of the right hand in bar 1 and also in bar 2 – with the aim of providing a slight emphasis on the second beat. Balancing the right-hand chords to the top will help to bring out the cheerful personality, and to shape the opening section into two four-bar phrases.

Bars 11–12 are perhaps the most awkward: the right hand will need detailed technical work with consistent fingering to achieve fluency. These bars, and the A major scale in bar 13, should also have musical shape and shading.

The surprising, mischievous change of personality from bar 17 is almost as if the dancers, exhausted by their jollities, are making a respectful goodbye. Phrasing should not be too literal here; instead, a more legato approach will underline the contrast in mood. To this end, it is important to hold down the left-hand crotchets under the quavers while bringing the melodic line to the fore.

The more teasing pianist may want to maintain the illusion with a cheeky ritardando in bars 21 to 22 before the final flourish towards the smiling appoggiatura at the end.

A:3 L. Kozeluch *Air cosaque*

The cross-armed, masculine feel of Cossack dances is not really reflected in this cheeky and comic song, but it has a huge jokey personality. Many humorous musical contrasts are encountered throughout; even in the first four bars there are two very distinct personalities at work, that of a boister-ous dancer, perhaps, and a cheeky joker. The more legato accompaniment of the second section builds to a merry punch-line. A slightly more risqué joke that draws cautious laughter is told in the third section, and the final section grows to a wonderfully astonished 'well I never' in bars 28 to 29. A little time taken across the B in bar 29 (the highest note of the piece) works wonders before the inevitable da capo.

Technical hurdles abound: the piece needs a confident range of articulation and control to encapsulate the character. Much of this musical detail should be educated into the fingers early on, while still in the earliest stages of learning the notes.

The opening staccato can be quite bright and confident, from the wrist but carefully controlled tonally so that it doesn't become too heavy. The contrasting *piano* is a staccato achieved from the surface of the keys. From bar 9 a smooth and unobtrusive accompaniment is required, making much of the crescendo towards bar 13, which calls for a bright and rhythmic right hand. Bars 17 and 18 will need some attention to ensure a true legato in the right hand's fingers, over a light and crisp left hand.

Finally, don't take the phrasing too literally in the final five bars before the da capo; a legato approach and perhaps a dab of pedal between the first two quavers of bar 32 will provide an effective contrast to the return of the main theme.

A:4 Beethoven *Bagatelle in A minor*

There are only nine bars to learn in this attractive, playful, but slightly melancholy waltz. Although a mere 'bagatelle' in name and length, it is quite sophisticated, demanding a maturity of understanding and an authority of control, together with subtlety of sound and rhythmic nuance.

Essential to the dance is the tempo and also an elegant left hand, which should be light on the chords with a dab of pedal on the first beat (taking off on the second). Thinking in a circular gesture will help encourage a down-and-up gesture of the arm and wrist from first to second beat, followed by a light caress of the hand on the third beat (for a soft end to the bar). The right hand glides across the keys with a gentle crescendo to the top C, a slight lift at the end of bar 3 perhaps, and then a *subito piano* for bar 4. Keeping the two harmony notes quiet below the A in bar 4 is crucial to help the soft tone.

Notational detail, though important, should be within the context of the piece's charm, style and dynamic. The *sforzando* may look significant but it is little more than a reminder to keep the tone full before the final *piano* chord. Similarly, the staccato 'wedges' in bars 9–11 are an indication to enhance the rest in the following bar. (A short, accented end to the right-hand phrase would be wholly inappropriate.)

The direction of *un poco sentimentale* indicates a natural rhythmic flexibility and spacing, so allowing a little time will enhance the ends of phrases and the sudden dynamic changes. Sustain the final chord no longer than its notated crotchet – a mere wave of a gloved hand.

A:5 Petzold *Bourrée*

This cheerful, sprightly bourrée, with its characteristic fourth-beat anacrusis and two-in-a-bar feel, dances delightfully through a number of echoed phrases and sequences in a predominantly two-part texture. It is not so simple to control or play as it perhaps sounds. Plenty of independent and separate learning of the hands is crucial, both to acquire sufficient control and to familiarize the fingers with the articulation and phrasing necessary to convey the piece's character and buoyancy.

The first four bars make up the first phrase: in bars 1 and 3 sensitive shaping is needed through the right hand's repeated notes, keeping the upbeat light and short. For bars 7 to 12 the music divides into shorter phrases, offering the opportunity for some terraced dynamics, alternating *forte* and *piano*. The quaver figures would respond well to a variety of articulation. In bar 5, for example, the first three quavers might be phrased together, with the rest detached. The thirds should be lightly voiced to the top note to avoid heaviness. Similar consideration can be given to the second half, but experimentation may lead to inspirational musical discussion and some imaginative alternatives.

It is easier and often more effective for the left hand to follow the articulation of the right; phrasing the first three notes together and matching the right hand's staccato at the end of the bar works well, detaching the following upbeat. There is no better way of working at essentially two-part pieces than as duets, focusing on the interplay between the parts while acquiring the co-ordination to put the hands together.

This is a challenging dance but is one that will live fresh in the fingers long after the exam.

A:6 Telemann *Allegretto in C*

On first hearing this coquettish piece it is not immediately obvious why it comes across as a little teasing. Looking at the phrase-lengths, however, one realizes how cleverly, and with what humour, Telemann plays with the audience's expectations. Gone is the almost mandatory first four-bar phrase; instead there are three, then two, then five bars – a surprise around every corner.

The problem lies not in playing the notes but in making the unexpected structure sound intentional. A convincing dynamic scheme and careful rhythmic playing are essential; this means in particular not just holding the dotted crotchets for their full length but allowing the tiniest of commas to indicate the end of the phrase. Bars 12 and 14 are awkward, for the descending jump requires careful negotiation and the quaver rest mustn't be clipped. Counting 1, 2, 3 aloud while playing these bars is the best way to feel the time available and avoid rushing or adding extra beats.

Articulation is relatively straightforward. You can choose whether to play the quavers in bar 2 and elsewhere detached, or to phrase the first two together, but in general hands match throughout. Dynamically a *piano* for the echo in bar 4 works well, as does a confident tone before the double bar and a crescendo through the ascending sequence in bars 25–30.

Don't be put off by the ornaments: the light grace notes (e.g. in bar 3) could be placed just before or on the beat; the trill in bar 10 and at the end is merely an upper mordent (and perhaps only needed in the right hand).

Above all, keep the performance simple and dance-like – and play with a smile, both literal and musical.

B:1 Grechaninov *Sad Song*

There is something about sad music that seems to touch even the youngest player.

This beautiful folk-style melody will require a singing right hand supported by light left-hand chords. The staccato should not be too short but more like pizzicato; it might be helpful to imagine that the singer is accompanied by the balalaika, a guitar-like Russian folk instrument.

The given fingering for the first theme appears unusual, but it does work and it keeps most of the notes under just one hand-position. However, there are two finger manoeuvres worth anticipating. In bar 2 move the right-hand fourth finger into position over the D in good time, and in bar 3 keep the hand relaxed as the thumb replaces the second on the F♯; it is very easy to slip off a black key.

There is only one dynamic mark given by the composer, but this piece clearly requires much more colour. The end of each four-bar phrase should fade a little. The middle section (in D major) requires a brighter mood, despite the left hand's B♭ hinting at the minor mode. Encourage your pupil to think of a scheme for the dynamics and write it into the score.

Without delaying the beat, allow a tiny breath at the end of each phrase. In bar 16 linger over the right hand's quaver F♯; it is both the last note of the phrase within a rallentando and the upbeat to the final phrase. Linger, too, over the unexpected D in bar 19. It creates a poignant dissonance, and the resulting falling 3rd at the cadence – which sounds rather like a sigh – also reveals the music's Slavic nature.

B:2 Korganov *Kleiner Walzer (Little Waltz)*

Compared to the other five pieces in List B the length of this little waltz may deter some pupils from even considering it. That would be a great pity because it is full of charm and character; one can almost see the dancers moving elegantly to its lilting phrases. Moreover, the last section (from bar 33) is a direct repeat of the first, and it lies very comfortably under the hands.

The first theme belongs to the ladies of the dance. Although the melody falls into four-bar phrases, these are subdivided into two by a crescendo and diminuendo shaping for each pair of bars, creating an undulating outline. The dotted minims of the left-hand accompaniment must be carefully sustained, especially when they move chromatically as in bars 3–6 and 11–14 where they form a significant melodic shape. Keep the crotchets quiet and shape them gracefully when slurred in pairs.

At bar 17 the gentlemen leap into the limelight with a more energetic theme in the left hand. Be positive about this change of character both with the dynamics and articulation, but resist any temptation to change the tempo. The suggested metronome mark (crotchet = *c*.126) is appropriate, but it would be better to feel it as one-in-a-bar.

There is little need for pedal in this piece – indeed its use could obscure expressive details and cause smudging – but a light touch from first to second beats in bars 16, 32 and 48 will join those slurred left-hand notes. Dynamic marks are plentiful and, if followed, should result in a colourful performance.

B:3 Schumann *Wilder Reiter (The Wild Horseman)*

Some of the most familiar and best-loved pieces for children are to be found among those written by Robert Schumann for his young family. This is one of the most exciting – a piece to stimulate the imagination. Is the horseman a messenger carrying urgent news or a highwayman riding out at night to intercept a stagecoach?

There may not be many notes to learn, but the piece is technically quite challenging and provides an excellent opportunity for developing staccato. A light forearm touch would be simplest for the melody lines, although hand (wrist) staccato would be equally effective if slightly more difficult to achieve. Most pianists find it easier to play with the right hand, so encourage extra practice for the left in the middle section until it matches the agility and articulation of the right. Some useful fingering is given, but if finger 2 is used on the second A in bar 1 (and similar) it not only creates a fingering sequence, it also helps to carry the hand upwards with the phrase.

Only one dynamic level (*mezzo-forte*) is given in the score, but some contrasts and nuances will be needed to create interest and give shape to the phrasing. For instance, there is a natural rise and fall to each four-bar phrase which can be highlighted with a slight crescendo and diminuendo. Be careful not to let the *sforzando* accents become too explosive; they are already marked by a slur in the right hand and a sustained crotchet chord in the left. The last phrase could either be bold and triumphant or fade away, as though the rider is disappearing into the darkness of the night.

B:4 Elgar *Enigma Theme*

There are two surprising things about the arrangement of this much-loved theme by Elgar. The first is that such a simple reduction can work so well; the second, that it requires so little use of the sustaining pedal.

What it will need is a warm, singing tone – this piece provides an excellent opportunity for pupils to develop their cantabile technique. The fleshy pad of the finger should be in contact with the key as the stroke begins, and arm weight applied gently to coax out the sound. Each one-bar segment of the main melody swells towards its middle note; this allows for a relaxation of the arm weight on the quieter fourth beat in preparation for the next bar. The rests that punctuate the theme add significantly to its expressive quality and must be given meticulous attention.

The middle section is just a little more flowing, and the challenge here is to produce a seamless line from left hand to right as the theme rises and increases in volume. The emotional climax occurs at bars 13 and 14 with the emergence of a counter-melody in the left hand, before the music gradually subsides to close on a glowing C major chord. Here it will be necessary to employ the sustaining pedal in order to retain the full harmony. The last two bars will feel very long, especially as the music has been slowing down, so careful counting is required here.

Dynamic marks have been generously supplied, but remember that melodies must sing, even at *piano*. It would be helpful to listen to the original orchestral version to gain some idea of the colour and sonority of this glorious melody.

B:5 Hugo Reinhold *Silhouette*

Its intriguing title may well promote some discussion, but there is no denying the charm and good humour of this character piece. However, with a dynamic range of *pianissimo* to only a little above *piano* it will require a delicate touch and neat fingerwork.

Use a little weight on each of the crotchets that are marked with lines and then lighten the arm for the staccato semiquavers and quavers that follow. The accompanying chords, whether they are in the left or the right hand, should be light and airy. The melody is played first by the right hand and then (in an altered version) by the left, so it is important that articulation matches as closely as possible. The slurred pairs of crotchets in bars 13–16 could have a tiny break between them. In bar 16 a *poco rit.* would not only alert the listener to the imminent return of the original theme, but make it easier to reposition the hands for this event. Here, too, the *una corda* pedal could be depressed and remain so until the end. In bar 21 look out for the accented diminished 7th chord that introduces a brief change of colour to the harmony and mood. As the music fades away, the sustaining pedal will be needed to hold the tied notes of the final chord. This will enable the left hand to glide gracefully over to take the final top note.

This dance-like piece does not want to feel rushed, and the composer's tempo, *Mäßig schnell* (moderately fast), suits a metronome mark of about crotchet = 72. For exam purposes, of course, the eye will have to get used to omitting the first-time bar.

B:6 Weber *Écossaise*

The écossaise is usually a lively, extrovert dance, but here the mood is more expressive. Perhaps the performance instruction *con tenerezza* (with tenderness) and dedication to the fair ladies in Hamburg indicates that the sixteen-year-old Weber was in love.

A careful study of the articulation will help to establish the shape of the phrasing, and an important feature is the descending line of suspensions that begins with the last quaver of bar 2. These syncopated, falling slurs carry a strong emotional message and must be lovingly shaped. The left hand's accompanying chords should be played as legato as possible.

The second half of this binary-form dance contains some technical challenges in the shape of written-out turns. It is essential that these are played lightly, with the arm well supported so as not to impede the fingers. As a preliminary exercise to establish the correct rhythm, omit the turn and play just three repeated quavers (A in bar 17 and D in bar 19). The turn itself might flow more easily with the fingering 2-4-3-2-3. However, in bars 23 and 31, the turn will require a different solution: using the thumb for the last note (G) will afford a more comfortable approach to the next pair of notes. At both of these cadence points, the F♯ crotchet has to be held; a slight upward movement of the wrist will help in making a smooth move into the next chord and through to the final note.

Bars 18–20 and 26–8 will require great attention: the leaps made by the right hand crossing the left in these passages should be practised slowly at first, so that the movement is relaxed and graceful. A slight *poco rit.* at the final cadence will bring this charming dance to a happy conclusion.

C:1 Christian Diendorfer *Tastenritt (Riding over the Keys)*

Technically straightforward, this piece (its title literally translated as 'Keyboard Ride') presents few obstacles – once the quirky harmonies and time changes have been sorted out.

The touch needs to be incisive and firm, to ensure that the chords and hands co-ordinate precisely. Little subtlety is required here, although the slurred markings between the semiquavers and dotted quavers must be observed. Avoid over-accenting the semiquaver, however, and encourage a sliding motion between the two notes. Although rhythmic complications are few, there might be a tendency to miscount the minim A at bar 4 and, after the time change, the rests in bar 18.

The music's character is slightly sinister but still robust and lively – the jerky movement of the piece might conjure up a ride on the dodgems at a fairground. The opening must be *tempo giusto*, like a brisk march, but the chords in the right hand need to be lighter in order to make the differentiation between *forte* and *mezzo-forte*. The music must have more lilt from bar 12 where the time changes to triple metre; the accents in the left hand will help to anchor this. The mood at this point is perhaps that of a merry-go-round. From bar 16 a crescendo, although not marked, would lead suitably into the change of metre at bar 18.

This would be an ideal choice for slightly nervous or tentative pupils, who might gain confidence from playing this as their first piece. Examiners will always accept pieces played in any order.

C:2 Alan Haughton *Stroll On*

This chill-out piece will certainly hold appeal for a large number of candidates, but will not necessarily suit all. A relaxed strolling tempo will be needed, as will an instinct for the swung style.

Although the dotted rhythms (notes and rests) will be swung, everything else should be played straight. The right hand is tuneful but the contours are a little angular, with some larger stretches for smaller hands. It is important to encourage lateral wrist movement here, in order to deter any jerkiness. For example, in bar 1 treat the A and G♯ like a pivot or hinge and ensure that the Cs are lightly articulated, not accented. There are some awkward intervals in bar 11, but the suggested fingering will help negotiate a smooth path. Again to prevent tension, a pliable, flexible wrist movement will be necessary. The slurred dotted-quaver and semiquaver figures which occur throughout the piece need a gentle lift on each semiquaver, but the crotchet must be sustained where the pairing occurs from semiquaver to crotchet, for example at bar 9.

There is plenty of opportunity for strong dynamic contrasts: if they can be persuasively incorporated into a stylish performance, the examiner will be ready with merit and distinction marks. The touch overall can be quite light, but more firmness is needed at bar 8 (left hand) to encourage the crescendo. The accents in bars 15, 16, 23, 25 and 26 will require a robust attack and the little notes at the beginning of bar 24 must be briskly played on the beat.

An easy-going and slightly cheeky performance will leave the examiner smiling with their feet a-tappin'.

C:3 Joni Mitchell *Both Sides Now*

This beautiful arrangement of the Joni Mitchell classic is a definite winner and will appeal to many pupils. The syncopated rhythms might look daunting at first, so listening to this lovely ballad would be a good introduction to this piece.

The lyrics (part provided in the footnotes) are highly descriptive and can be used to stir the imagination. If trying to match up the words with this arrangement, you will find that the second stanza goes back to bar 1 (with an imaginary upbeat for 'But . . .') and the third stanza of lyrics corresponds to bar 9 (with the notated upbeat).

Good legato control and cantabile tone are essential, especially in the melodic line. The other parts should be gently supportive. Discourage a tendency to over-accent the thumbs. The fingering suggestions in bars 3 and 14 – where the finger is changed on the same note – will help to achieve fluid legato control.

The piece must always be played rhythmically but not rigidly; despite some angular intervals the phrases need to be pliable and shapely. Dynamics are restricted, maybe to convey the haunting quality of Joni's voice, but the important word here is *espressivo*.

Pedalling would enhance the performance for those students who are able and confident. Employ legato pedalling on the first and third beats in bars 1–4 and 7–12; omit pedal in bars 5 and 6, and lift the pedal on beat 4 of bar 8 to accommodate the quaver rest. Refrain from using pedal in bars 13–15 to avoid smudging, and then from bar 16 to bar 18 change the pedal in each bar on the first beat and on the tied quaver; in the last bar delay pedalling until the unexpected 9th chord (Eb/G) has sounded. The effect of this final harmony is wonderfully unresolved and questioning.

C:4 John Rowcroft *Triple Blues*

To swing or not to swing is answered simply here. Try the piece through with quavers played straight and then again giving them a gentle swing. The first option feels rather staid; the second conveys the Blues style more convincingly and also complies with the composer's direction. Certainly, to achieve those top marks the swung version is to be recommended, and it will certainly have more appeal for those students who enjoy this genre. However, it is important to aim for consistency here, even on the synco-pated quavers.

The mood and style are paramount. The piece should have a cool, laid-back feel and it will play itself once the notes are sorted. It is crucial to avoid accents and work towards good blending between the hands. The staccato chords and single notes are best if lightly detached, whereas the slurred, paired quavers should be smoothly tapered with just a gentle lift on the second quaver.

Dynamic markings are sparse but, as the opening *mezzo-forte* would indicate, the approach does not want to be too tentative. The melodic fragments need to have a little dominance over the chords, and this requires careful control of the balance. A crescendo is implied with the modulation into bar 18. Maintain a strong level here, in order to give the diminuendo in the last four bars greater impact. Pull back slightly in the penultimate bar – the piece wants to finish with a whisper, but an audible one.

C:5 M. Tajčević *Allegretto scherzando*

This characterful folk-like piece is from a collection by the Croatian composer Tajčević called *Songs from Mur Island*. To convey its playful mood a lively tempo and a buoyant rhythmic approach will be needed.

The rhythms are straightforward but there might be a tendency to hurry bars 9–16, where the syncopated left hand is combined with the crescendo. These bars should be practised firstly with left-hand chords on the beat, then with the split figuration (as used in bar 27) and then finally with the more challenging offbeat rhythms. Tapping both hands on a surface, without the distraction of the notes, would help to tighten up the rhythmic sense. Remember, it is perfectly acceptable for candidates with small hands to adapt chords that they find too far to stretch; here, this would apply to the left hand in bars 2, 4, 6 and 8 (second chord) and possibly also bar 25.

The staccato touch must be crisp and incisive. The tenuto mark on almost every crotchet, however, implies that the note should be fully sustained but not over-accented. The piece is full of opportunities for vivid dynamic contrasts, which the examiner will expect to hear (especially for those merit and distinction marks). Some use of direct pedalling might also add colour, for example depressing the pedal on the second beat of bar 20, lifting immediately with the first beat of bar 21; the same could apply with bars 22–3, and in bar 24 but this time holding down the pedal until the second beat of bar 26.

The ritardandos, tempo changes and pause marks are subtle and need careful planning. At bar 16 the quaver movement is reminiscent of an engine slowing down. The pause mark between bars 16 and 17 means complete silence before the dreamy and reflective *Meno mosso*. A precisely counted bar's rest will add drama and tension at bar 35, then after a thoughtful moment the piece finishes with a teasing and energetic two bars.

C:6 Karen Tanaka *Northern Lights*

The composer's footnotes give plenty of food for thought, and looking at some spectacular photographs of the aurora borealis will be further inspiration. The student must use both visual imagery and imagination in order to give a persuasive account of this evocative piece, which might not be the right choice for everybody. Listening is the key to a successful performance, and gaining experience of playing on different pianos will be invaluable, as the touch and the pedal can vary so much.

A fluid, light and transparent-like touch will be needed in the right hand to create an almost hypnotic and mystical atmosphere. The left hand requires a good sense of keyboard geography as well as the ability to cross over the right hand without disturbing the flow. The 5ths in the treble would benefit from a gentle yet glittering tone, like shimmering stars, but those in the bass should have a quiet, sustained resonance.

The pedal creates some magical effects, and at the end, where it must be left on to suggest infinity, both performer and audience can luxuriate in the overtones. The pedalling itself will not present difficulty but it is worth delaying the depression of the pedal until at least the second quaver of the bar, and in some acoustics the third.

To gain confidence initially, the notes need to be played quite firmly and not too quietly; eventually, however, quite a wide spectrum is achievable within these softer shades. The quintuple time, although perhaps a little off-putting at first, will not be problematic if the left-hand chords are precisely synchronized with the quavers in the right. The overall impression should be one of timelessness, so it is important to avoid accentuation on the first beat of the bar. Although not usually expected in the exam, consider observing the repeat marks between bars 18 and 21, to complement the structure of the first section and give a better balance to the ending.

GRADE 4

Many of the List B pieces will benefit from some pedal, but if your pupil's legs are too short there is always an alternative piece from the extensive lists. The musical character of candidates often becomes more firmly established at this stage and they can play to their strengths, making sure the pieces are contrasted in tempo and mood.

A:1 Anon. *Allegro in F*

If this piece by an unknown composer was selected by Leopold Mozart for his daughter to study, you can be sure of its pedagogical value – but it is also good fun to play. It is musically uncomplicated; once the notes are thoroughly known it will flow comfortably under the fingers.

With its continuous semiquaver movement, the music will require crisp articulation and evenness of delivery, for which your pupil needs a reliable left hand that can match the right in agility. In order to cultivate the brilliance of finger attack that is appropriate to the character of this music, try a little exercise on a flat surface and listen to the fingers tapping. They do not have to be lifted very far off the surface to achieve the desired result. It is rather like drumming the fingers impatiently, only in an even and controlled way.

For the most part the supporting quavers sound effective if they are detached, but a few slurs can add interest. In bars 5 and 6 a slur on the second beat gives a lift to the cadence, and the same should then be observed in bars 11, 15 and 16. Don't be put off by the ornaments in bars 7 and 8: they are turns, and the suggested interpretation is simple and unfussy.

Some dynamic marks are given, but there is no reason why a few more should not be added. Allow the shape of the phrasing and the way in which the figures rise and fall to suggest what might work, and if your pupil can come up with some ideas on the subject, so much the better.

A:2 J. C. F. Bach *Scherzo*

As the title suggests, this is a good-humoured, rather playful piece which will appeal to the extrovert pianist. There are some technical challenges, though, and nimble fingers and secure co-ordination will be needed.

It is debatable whether the semiquavers in bar 2 (and similar) should be divided into slurred pairs, for the result could turn out to be jerky when played up to speed. There are not many slurs in the piece and they may have been intended as bowing marks (a common practice of the period); nevertheless, the musical result of playing the slurred quavers as indicated (e.g. bars 13 and 14) is quite attractive. Quavers without slurs can be lightly detached to give energy.

To fit the trills (bars 14 and 18) with the left-hand quavers, first think of them as groups of 3 + 4, ending the trill on the third quaver of the bar. Later they should fall evenly into place. If the timing of the ornament in bar 16 proves troublesome, try sounding the tied note of the suggested realization until the ear gets used to hearing where the second demisemiquaver goes.

When hands play semiquavers together, listen carefully to the co-ordination, and especially to the timing of the left hand in bar 9. It might help to hear this passage in sequences of four notes beginning with the right hand's E-D-C-D then the left hand's entry in canon with the same notes.

Once the technical detail is comfortably under control, the dual nature of the music will begin to emerge. It is as though there are two characters. The first is energetic and irrepressible (passages marked *forte*), the second more serious and thoughtful (*piano*) – naturally, it is the chatterbox who has the last word!

A:3 Beethoven *Minuet in G*

The charm and affable nature of this minuet will make it a popular choice. Only the technique of managing the double notes – 3rds and 6ths – and the dotted rhythms will present any real challenges.

The suggested fingering which enables a smooth flow for these double notes will take a little time to master. Some of the fingering may be new to pupils (e.g. in bar 1, using 5/1 on white notes and 4/2 on the black) but this is a valuable combination that will be used time and again. In bars 9 and 13 another important fingering technique is employed. Intervals here are wider, and the thumb has to play consecutive notes. The trick is to play the top notes absolutely legato while gliding the thumb gently from note to note. Even if pedal is used, it is still better to play legato with the fingers.

The dotted rhythm is a key feature for this minuet: on no account must this figure slacken into a triplet rhythm. In this first section the accompanying crotchets could be slightly detached as though played by a cello.

The *sforzando* marks should not be overdone; they merely indicate accents, often placed on unexpected notes (e.g. in bars 5, 14 and 15).

In contrast to this section the trio glides smoothly in quavers, and to reinforce this effect you might like to keep the left hand legato as well. The phrase marks seem to break the melody at each bar-line, but, in common with a lot of music at this time, these should be regarded as bowing marks. Slurs should only be taken literally in places such as bars 25–8 where a repeated sequence requires shaping, and for pairs of notes like those in bar 30.

A:4 W. F. Bach *Aria in G minor*

The plaintive lyricism of this aria by the eldest of Bach's sons makes it an appealing alternative piece for List A.

The right hand carries the principal melody, but the left hand's counter-melody is just as important. While it should never dominate, the left hand must be given its own special identity. The piece could easily be played by violin and cello, or oboe and bassoon, and this idea may stimulate your pupil's imagination to create a good balance.

Given the song-like character of the music, the suggested articulation works well, with slurs indicating a predominantly legato outline. These slurs are more like bowing marks, so it is not necessary to lift the hand and leave a gap between every group. Quavers without slurs can be lightly detached – for instance, the upbeats at beginnings of phrases, and some of the left-hand patterns at/or approaching cadences (bars 4 and 7–8). The suggested dynamics will help to give colour and shape, especially to the sequences in bars 9–12 and 19–24. In the second of these sequences, in bars 19, 21 and 23, shorten the first-beat crotchet a little and add a slight stress to the following tied crotchet in order to mark the syncopation.

For the confident pupil, a few ornaments will make a stylish addition. On the last note of the first section a mordent (D-C♯-D) or the more expressive appoggiatura (quavers C♯ and D) would be easy to play. The ending can be similarly decorated. As the opening two-bar figure is repeated several times, a mordent could also be added to the first-beat quaver in bars 27 and 31.

A metronome mark of crotchet = 66–72 will allow the music an unhurried flow and sense of style.

A:5 Kuhlau *Vivace*

This is one of the most familiar and popular movements from the sonatina repertoire of the Classical period. It lies comfortably under the hands and encourages the development of finger technique and agility.

During the early stages of learning it would be helpful to get to know the form. For instance, practice could begin by working on all the appearances of the rondo theme (upbeats into bars 1, 37, and 77) and noticing what differences occur. Then look at the two appearances of the second theme (upbeats into bars 17 and 85) and discuss what key they are in and why the tonality is different the second time. This passage contains chromatic scales, and in some editions (including the ABRSM edition) you may find a fingering that employs the fourth finger. Although this alternative is frequently used, your pupil might still be struggling to remember the basic pattern, in which case it would be better to stick to that.

There is a change of mood and key signature for the central episode, and the former extrovert brilliance now gives way to a more lyrical, flowing theme. The left hand should be kept at a *pianissimo* level, fingers close to the keys, while the melody sings sweetly above. Dynamic marks should be carefully observed throughout the piece, but the *sforzando* marks must always be confined to the prevailing dynamic level.

For the closing section, instead of yet another appearance of the rondo theme, the movement ends with a sparkling Coda (upbeat into bar 105). However, it will quickly be noticed that this seemingly new tune starts with an inverted version of the Rondo theme's first two bars. Such is the ingenuity of the composer.

A:6 Mozart *Polonoise in D*

From as early as the sixteenth century the polonaise was a firm favourite of the aristocracy. The splendidly dressed dancers moved in procession around the ballroom, dipping and gliding to the characteristic rhythms of the music.

Mozart's polonoise (the spelling varies according to country or district) clearly shows these distinguishing rhythms. The opening bars contain the divided first beat (quaver and two semiquavers), and more emphasis should be placed on the second half of the beat. This is heard even more definitely at bars 5 and 6 where the grace note adds its own accent, and in bar 11 where the syncopation is obvious. At the end of each section the cadences have the typical strong second beat and lighter third.

Stylish articulation and dynamics are provided. The wedges over some notes are staccato marks, but crotchets will require more length than quavers to avoid a clipped effect. The turn in bar 9 is best included in the first crotchet beat; divide it into quaver + triplet semiquavers (F#-E-D), leaving four quavers (E-G-F#-A) to complete the bar. This solution not only fits comfortably with the left hand, but also provides the characteristic rhythmic impetus to the second half of the first beat.

The descending slurs in bar 3 could all be played with fingers 3-2 or by alternating 3-2 and 4-3. Whatever is chosen, the effect must be light and buoyant. The leap for the left hand in the same bar is not difficult once the notes have been pinpointed, but it may be necessary to snatch a glance at the keyboard to be sure of a safe landing!

B:1 Carroll *Alone at Sunset*

Walter Carroll's own thoughts combined with the evocative quotation from Shelley give us an incredibly vivid musical picture (see footnotes). Here it will be essential to have imagination, a real connection with the Romantic style, and an artist's palette. However, this may be just the piece for a student who needs encouraging in these attributes!

The undulating roll of the sea can be clearly pictured in the left-hand figuration (bars 1–8) and here the phrases should be felt in four-bar lengths. However, the phrasing of bars 9–24 is irregular (bars 9–10 together, then 11–13, 14–19 and 20–24), which gives an expressive build-up to the climax in bar 17 (third beat). The sunset then disappears from the horizon and the last eight bars leave us with a warm nostalgic glow.

The music needs to ebb and flow, making this an ideal opportunity to introduce rubato. For example, you could give a sense of forward motion from bar 14 through to the end of bar 18 – but taking a little time over the third beat of bar 17. It is important, however, that the rubato is felt and not imposed.

The pianist can luxuriate in the pedalling, which is straightforward and clearly marked. The desired sound-world is created by a velvety and warm tone, with perhaps a lighter touch adopted for the notes marked with a staccato. The final wash of sound from the pedal held over the last four bars should be fully savoured.

Your pupil would find it worthwhile to look at a sunset over water to see the myriad of different colours and depths it produces. If this can be only partially matched in the music the result will be both effective and rewarding.

B:2 Kabalevsky *Waltz*

This delightful, if slightly quirky, waltz requires a calm and gentle approach, especially in order to accommodate the tricky leaps. Compared with the Romantic waltzes of Chopin, Kabalevsky's waltz is more metronomic, less lyrical.

Since good keyboard geography is needed it will be essential to start with separate-hands practice. Negotiating the precipitous left-hand intervals in particular requires careful and slow work. One practice technique (omitting pedal in bars 1–2) is to insert a rest in-between each note or chord so that the following note is covered before it is played. Restore the correct notation once notes can be accurately and confidently played, without looking down at the keys. Moving from second to third beats in bar 1 needs a lateral movement in the left hand, for which the fourth finger acts like a pivot or hinge. After this is mastered, direct pedalling can be added, and this will increase the sense of security.

Don't be surprised if there are some wobbly moments when the hands are put together. Fingering for the right-hand 6ths, especially for those with a larger stretch, could be: 5/2, 4/1 (bars 1–2); 5/2, 5/1, 4/1 (bars 3–4); and the given fingering in bars 7–8.

At the *un poco più mosso* (bar 9) the phrasing is interesting – it is like blowing up a balloon, beginning with short breaths for the two-bar phrases before increasing the flow until reaching the expansive and expressive eight-bar phrase (bars 17–24). Encouraging students to think of the breath flow will also deter them from over-accenting the third beat. The left-hand accompaniment at this point should imitate dry pizzicato strings.

Finally, place the last two chords carefully, taking a little extra time so that the *pianissimo* notes are audible.

B:3 Maikapar *Chez le forgeron (At the Smithy)*

To introduce this energetic and delightful piece, describe or imagine a blacksmith hard at work: hammers against metal; sparks flying; iron sizzling in cold water.

It is quite straightforward, once some ground rules have been laid concerning the placement of overlapping hands in the outer sections (bars

1–20 and 34–47). The metronome indication is just right but the tempo ultimately must be dictated by the semiquavers, which should be incisive and clear. Since there might be a tendency to rush the dotted beats in bars 7–10 (and wherever that pattern occurs), students should count carefully.

The voicing of chords should also have consideration. Try to encourage a singing top line. Pupils will enjoy the *martellato* effect at the beginning but must also incorporate the accents clearly. The imitative figurations in the first part of the middle section (bars 21–8) could be the sparks flying from the anvil; attentive pointing and balancing of entries will be required here.

The pedalling may need to be varied for different acoustics or pianos: experiment by changing the pedal every bar in bars 1–4, 11–14 and so on. Although the pedal may be omitted in bars 21–8 for a more energetic result, it will certainly be required from bar 29 when the student can really savour the rolling motion of the quavers.

This is a super piece, and it provides the opportunity for an evocative and engaging performance. Once mastered, it will present little problem in the exam room.

B:4 Berlioz *Hungarian March*

Quite a brisk tempo (crotchet = 140) is needed for this famous march, which will have appeal for many students. The arrangement is straight-forward, presenting few challenges. However, an alert sense of rhythm and imagination will be required in order to project the character and the necessary orchestral colours.

Listening to a recording or, better still, following the music with an orchestral score would be a good starting-point. A clear, crisp and light touch will be needed to imitate the woodwind (which are prominent throughout), with a warm firm tone especially at bars 7 and 28 to conjure up the strings at this point. The accent marks need positive projection, particularly at bar 8 where the cymbal puts in an appearance.

The articulation that has been clearly marked also mirrors the full score, but the left hand at bars 3–6, 11–14 and 21–5 might be played with a light, semi-legato touch. The dynamics are quite definite, offering sudden contrasts of colour, but a small crescendo is perhaps advisable in bars 7–8. To prevent the balance between the hands from being a little bottom-heavy, the right hand will require lots of bright, zingy articulation.

Rhythms must be meticulous and taut throughout. Miscounting or rushing the tied notes might be problematic; this applies especially in bars

28–9 and 32–3 where it is vital to feel the third and first beats strongly – bars 18–19 also need to be carefully counted. However, slow and measured practice from the beginning will give confidence, which in turn should lead to an assured performance in the exam room.

B:5 Chaminade *Idyll*

Imagine rowing leisurely down a river on a warm summer's day, in a bucolic setting – and you will have captured the right mood for this charming piece.

It certainly needs to be 'very flowing' but the *bien chanté* is a reference to the cantabile that is required. Although every note must sing, care should be taken not to over-accentuate, especially on the second of the dotted crotchets. Enjoy the arching contours but think of the phrases in four rather than two bars. The shape of the phrase lends itself to a natural crescendo and decrescendo, but the touch initially should not be too tentative. Perhaps because of a change in the weather or the swell from a passing boat, the middle section beginning at the upbeat into bar 17 is slightly more turbulent, and yet the cheerful mood prevails. The tone can be brighter here and the bloom of the phrase more intense, but the left hand's dotted crotchets in bars 17–20 and 25–30 should be carefully sustained in order to support the right hand.

The pedal, as well as helping the harmonic outline, will give fluency, add tonal warmth, and project an overall sense of lyricism. Do ensure that the three quavers beginning each phrase are clear and not pedalled. When playing with pedal on an unfamiliar instrument or in a strange acoustic, the need to listen acutely cannot be overemphasized – inattentive pedalling can hamper an otherwise diligently prepared performance.

Treat the acciaccatura in bar 15 as a lightly articulated semiquaver placed before the beat. During the da capo, the *poco rit.* from bar 14 (second beat) brings the boat trip to a satisfactory conclusion – remember to avoid slowing down in the same bars on the first time through.

B:6 Hugo Reinhold *Scherzo*

A gentle one-in-a-bar tempo gives the music its necessary lilt and suits the character of both the scherzo and the dance-like trio. Agility and careful fingering are needed to achieve clarity in the opening repeated-quaver motif. Using the printed 3-2-1 fingering on the quaver Cs at bar 1 and similar is recommended, but preliminary fingerwork away from the keyboard might also be beneficial. The springy octave leaps from bar 9 are fun but need precise placing. A bright lift onto the higher octave note will emphasize the *fz*, but this must not be overly forced.

The scherzo will exude an appropriately playful air if the contrasts between slurs and staccato are well projected. Avoid the tendency to over-accent the third beats in bars 6 and 7 (also 22 and 23); they need no extra stress.

The trio has the feel of a ländler (a waltz-like folk dance). The melodic conversation between the hands needs expressive shape, with careful balancing of the other parts. Discreet dabs of pedal will add warmth in bars 25, 29, 33 and 37 (between first and second beats), but the right-hand quaver rests – like a short intake of breath – must not be obscured. Sustain the dotted minims in the inner and lower parts using legato fingering, as too much pedal might blur the lines. Bars 35–6 are a little awkward, as it is difficult to sustain the E in the left-hand chord: fingering 2-1-2-3-5-3/2 in the right hand, taking the left hand's G# and A with the right-hand thumb, is an alternative fingering, which might suit those who can stretch a 7th.

The usual rule about omitting repeats applies here, but the da capo after the trio will be expected.

C:1 A. Benjamin *Soldiers in the Distance*

This evocative and imaginative piece may well be familiar to some teachers from their youth, as it makes a welcome reappearance to Grade 4 after more than 40 years.

The marching left-hand 5ths, a consistent lightness of touch, and precise yet light staccato will undoubtedly be a challenge. However, once these technical considerations and the tonal control are comfortable the piece almost plays itself. All that remains is some subtle dynamic shading of the right-hand melody and a fearless level of rhythmic precision.

Be wary of the composer's suggestion of 'red-hot keys', which could lead to physical tension. The staccato is achieved from the surface of the key with the fingers, but without following the key right down to the key bed – make just a quick brush of the key's surface with a little weight, as if flicking off a speck of dust. Since the exam piano may be unfamiliar, opt for a dynamic a little more than the suggested *pianissimo* at the start, making a diminuendo into bar 2 as fingers get used to the weight and touch.

Overall the right hand should be tonally more positive than the left, particularly at the beginnings of phrases. In this way, a decrescendo may accompany the descending sequence without ending up too soft on the tied notes. As the composer points out, these tied notes should be loud enough to sustain over the top of the marching feet.

Bars 22–4 require more technical work than the rest: fingers must be immaculately co-ordinated and rhythmically stable. To enhance the disappearance of the soldiers at the end, start the final 'muffled' drumbeats slightly louder, then bring the dynamic down. Remember to count the rests rigorously, and to hold the hand above the keys for the final three-beat rest.

C:2 Gillock *Carnival in Rio*

There is a real feel-good factor about this festive piece, which is slightly reminiscent of the final movement 'Brazileira' of Milhaud's *Scaramouche* – a useful comparison. In order to absorb the idiom of a Rio carnival it is well worth internalizing the characteristic Latin rhythm that pervades the piece.

The form divides neatly into A–B–A + Coda, with the most deceptively tricky moments being in the middle section. The placing of the chords is crucial here yet the left hand may have a mind of its own. Start by separating the right hand into phrases of 3+3+2 semiquavers to help the co-ordination, keeping the left-hand chords short, and then join the phrases together as marked – some teacher/pupil duet practice will help consolidate this.

The outer sections rely heavily on the articulation and a very firm sense of pulse. The phrasing and articulation of both hands should be exactly as marked; detach the final note of each right-hand phrase, although the left hand's staccato crotchets should be a little longer than the following staccato quavers. The suggested tempo is excellent – any faster and the cheek and humour of the piece would be lost.

Few dynamics are marked but the opening right-hand melody does need some dynamic shading within this, growing as the scale ascends (the left hand keeps out of the way). Bars 9 to 24 rely more on the harmonic and rhythmic interest, so here the left hand can lend a little more tonal support. There should be the most dramatic and effective contrast possible at bar 17.

Enjoy the surprise ending, which needs to be played with conviction. Allow the preceding diminuendo to reach a dramatic extreme to enable a bold, colourful and vibrant end.

C:3 Hengeveld *Blues*

From the composer of numerous teaching gems this is a smooth, smoochy number that will appeal strongly to pupils while cleverly offering a technical challenge. It may seem like an easy piece of pastiche jazz, but the slow tempo and the legato required to convey the melancholy, vocal character will demand and also reward careful study.

Pedalling the piece would be too complex at this level, as the changes are too frequent. Fortunately pedal is not really needed; the legato required to avoid any harmonic confusion must come from the fingers. Creating this legato is both a listening and a physical skill that is well worth developing.

With or without pedal, legato 3rds in the left hand are crucial. Practise playing just the first two 3rds; deliberately overlap all four notes and listen to the overlap before releasing the first of the two pairs. Continue with the next until the control of the release of the preceding 3rds is both conscious and a true legato. Despite the phrasing, consider joining all the left-hand 3rds in bar 2 as well. Once the physical control is there, focus on achieving a gentle, unobtrusive tone to underpin the melody. Note that in bars 5 and 6 it is important to hold the semibreves under the minims.

Over this the 'call and response' right-hand melody needs to be equally legato and dynamically shaped, again without taking the phrasing too literally. All dotted rhythms should be played as a swung triplet, and the triplet figures in bar 12 'stretched' for added expression.

A bold contrast for the middle section is wholly appropriate as is a slight holding-back of the final bass note – the only place where a dab of pedal is essential to warm the tone.

C:4 Detlev Glanert *Lied im Meer (Song in the Sea)*

There are few students who couldn't be beguiled into playing this song, especially if they hear their teacher give a musically subtle rendition of it. Full of watery depth and mystery, it is a wonderfully pictorial piece, which offers the opportunity to explain the importance of imagery in music and how it relates to the evocative sound-world.

The initial *piano* needs to be interpreted not just as soft but in its more literal, Italian sense of 'gently, slowly'; the key to the atmosphere and musical effectiveness lies in the time taken through the rests, which should always be counted correctly and given their full length, particularly in the empty bars where the pedal's resonance captures the colours of the deep. Counting in thousands (1000, 2000 etc.) can help avoid clipping the beats.

At bar 13 the waters flow with more purpose and the song begins, eventually accompanied by a full-bodied, deeply swelling, crashing sea. Effective balance through these bars is crucial; the left-hand 4ths and 5ths need to build gently without interfering with the melody, and the right-hand chords should then be carefully graded to provide the diminuendo in bar 21. The pedal change in bar 14 holds the F♯ grace note, whether the note is played with or before the left-hand chord. In bar 22 the tune moves to the tenor register where it is even more important to keep the chords light and out of the way.

The overall tempo should be not too slow but gently moving, so that a gradual ritardando through the final bars is possible without the sea becoming frozen over!

This is an absorbing, captivating and colourful piece that will enrich a developing musician.

C:5 Michael Rose *Habanera*

Some preparatory listening will be helpful (and indulgent) here. Introduce the Latin habanera character to your student as you both enjoy the famous aria from Bizet's *Carmen* or Ravel's *Habanera* – which has an identical opening.

The distinctive rhythm, with its semiquaver almost delayed too much, characterizes this somewhat seductive dance – the song-like nature of which needs to be conveyed through subtle control of the balance and sound, as well as enticing dynamic shading (follow the hairpins decisively).

The melody begins on a shared F♯. Contrary to what is indicated, take this with the right hand, second finger, and then in bar 4 use the right hand's thumb on the A; alternatively, make absolutely sure that the A is projected well enough to be heard as the last note of the melodic line. The left-hand melody should have sufficient rich tone and musical shape for its personality to come across. The dotted habanera motif must always be beautifully soft in the background; it is therefore crucial that the performer changes the touch for these moments, for instance in bars 13–14 (both hands) and 17–18.

The triplets should be expansive and the pedal changed gently in order to create a seamless but evocative sound-world. Avoid becoming too distracted by the articulation detail; in bar 19, for instance, the staccato marks imply a rhythmic edge to the sound while pedalled, not a dry articulation. In bars 21–3 pedal is still required but it needs to be changed more often, particularly in bar 23. In bar 34 interpret the tenuto not only literally but also as an opportunity for a slight ritenuto, holding back in anticipation of the surprising kiss in bar 35. Savour the pause! The final bars might be a fraction slower with much less pedal as the final chord is approached.

C:6 Shostakovich *Clock-work Doll*

This characterful and cleverly descriptive piece will attract the younger pianists. Although relatively straightforward musically (with virtually no rhythmic pliancy required to convey the clockwork image), it needs good independence of hands, tidy fingers, and attention to the details of articulation and dynamics.

As the piece is, essentially, in two independent parts, learning it separate-hands is advisable. Give particular focus to the left hand, which needs to develop good technical and rhythmic control, to ensure that it has as much personality as the right. The phrases must contain more than a dry, crisp staccato by adding a musical shading. Overall the phrase shapes are fairly obvious, but within it various options are possible. For example, the right hand grows to the top G in the first two bars with the second beat then shaded away. The next phrase could be considered as either a two-bar echo of the first or the beginning of a six-bar phrase that rises to the top B before falling down to the end of the phrase.

Contrasts of dynamic are important, and these will affect the way in which the staccato is achieved. This will mostly be with the fingers and from the key's surface but the *forte* in bars 13–14 requires a stronger action from the wrist. From bar 18 the doll begins a rather strange dance: with the musical interest alternating between the hands here, the balance will need clear definition. The doll appears to wind down from bar 26 but, given an abrupt 'flick with the finger' in bar 29, continues to dance until, swirling in circles, it falls down in a heap in the final bar, so no ritardando is needed.

GRADE 5

School exams often become a serious threat to practice around Grade 5, so forward planning is helpful to ease the pressure. The preparation time for this grade will need to be longer than for the previous grades, but some light pieces that are quick to absorb will help to maintain enjoyment in playing while the exam work is being systematically covered.

A:1 J. S. Bach *Air*

This majestic piece is a good choice for a disciplined pupil with proficient facility in both hands. The quaver movement is distributed between the two hands and the wide right-hand leaps need confidence and courage.

Reliable, systematic quaver fingering, securely in the memory, is essential if stumbles are to be avoided in performance. There are a number of difficult 'corners' in the left-hand part, so learning that hand alone may be a good starting-point.

The two-in-a-bar time signature, together with the gavotte-like phrasing, gives an airiness to the rhythm provided that the crotchets are kept light and buoyant. Although the technical demands (which include the semiquavers in bar 28b) will partly dictate the eventual tempo, remember that vitality is produced by a combination of factors – only one of which is speed.

The tone in the first half needs to be firm and confident, yet not ponderous. Detached crotchets and unslurred quavers will convey harpsichord-like brilliance, and the right-hand slurs in bars 8–10, which imply detached third and fourth quavers of each group, may also be applied to the other hand. The imitation at the start means a quieter tone in the right hand when the left hand begins the quavers, and the trill in bar 3 may be modified to a four-note turn, if necessary.

The more sustained texture of the right hand provides a change of mood after the double bar. Some finger substitution, as suggested, is needed to hold down the tied melodic notes, and quavers may be played more smoothly at this point; practising the upper notes without the underlying minims, using the same fingering, may prove beneficial here. Both sets of terraced dynamics will be effective if the *piano*s are sufficiently quiet, and bars 24–7 may require memorizing in order that the right-hand strides over the keyboard are negotiated accurately. Momentum should not be lost in the semiquavers in bar 28b and a well-paced ritardando will round off the piece with satisfaction.

A:2 J. H. Fiocco *Andante*

Here is an exquisite piece to be cherished by a musical pupil who is able to sustain the long melodic lines with all the sensitivity of a top-class violinist or oboist. While it may appear an easy option due to its leisurely pace and relative lack of intricacy, a really fine performance is dependent on subtle musical shaping, control of textures and well-integrated ornaments.

The left hand's quaver chords may give the impression of four beats in a bar, but thinking in two will allow the phrases to flow without intrusive accents. The triplets should be unhurried and evenly spaced. Playing the non-triplet semiquavers as *notes inégales*, as suggested, produces a gentle rocking rhythm, not dissimilar to swung jazz rhythms. Careful preparation of the ornaments, which should be placed on (not before) the beat, will ensure that they fit easily into the melodic line.

Pedalling, always controversial in this style of music, is a subject about which examiners keep an open mind, provided that its use does not spoil the melodic and harmonic clarity and it is musically convincing. Although it is possible to give a convincing performance without using pedal, selective dabs will enhance the left-hand legato, in addition to sustaining the ties onto repeated notes. As always, however, the ear is the best guide to making musical decisions.

The right-hand part can be divided into four main phrases – albeit long, intricate ones – with rests indicating breathing spaces. The suggested dynamics indicate the broad overall shape; for instance, the terraced levels in bars 13–18 reflect the rising sequences. Right-hand tone needs gentle shaping throughout to convey the undulating melodic contours. The tied notes, which always occur in the same place in the bar, can be given slight emphasis to convey their expressive qualities. The left-hand accompaniment needs careful balancing, but its own musical interest – the clashes in bars 10–11, for instance – should not be overlooked.

A:3 Haydn *Menuet and Trio*

Haydn's music is the product of a lively mind, quick-witted and often quirky, for although it seems to encapsulate the elegance of eighteenth-century life at Court, it is always full of unexpected twists. An effective performance of this pair of dance movements relies on good rhythmic control and a well-developed tonal sense.

The tempo of the menuet should be flowing yet unhurried, with the triplets and semiquavers evenly spaced in order to maintain a firm crotchet pulse. Omitting the ornaments initially is often wise – do not be afraid to modify them if the suggested realizations prove troublesome.

A firm *forte* tone and clearly defined dotted rhythms are needed at the opening. In contrast, the following three two-bar phrases, which may be slightly separated, need a more gentle and smooth approach. Tapered phrase-endings here and elsewhere will avoid unwanted third-beat accents. A slight crescendo through the triplets, taking care not to rush, will give direction towards the following bar. The *forte* that ends each half-section re-establishes the assuredness of the opening and the two-note semiquaver slurs provide an elegant detail. Bars 15–18 may need extra work in order to fit in the ornaments neatly and lightly. Left-hand phrasing here is a matter of personal preference, but in bar 18 and elsewhere detached crotchets suggest cello or bassoon articulation. Note the synchronization of the triplets in bar 23 and the footnote to play the final four bars twice in the reprise after the trio section.

This middle section (to be played at the same speed) is generally more straightforward rhythmically, although care is needed to space the triplets evenly. Reducing the trill in bar 36 to eight semiquavers may be a more manageable option for some. Most phrases are six bars in length and need their own dynamic level. There is plenty of scope for tonal inflection within phrases, and attention should be paid to the subtle suspensions created by the right hand's syncopated ties.

A:4 T. A. Arne *Presto*

The freshness and uncomplicated textures of this cheerful piece make it an attractive alternative choice. There are few ornaments to negotiate and figuration usually fits comfortably under the hand.

A *presto* marking can cause many candidates to play as fast as possible, often with disastrous consequences. Therefore, although there should certainly be a two-in-a-bar buoyancy to the gigue-like dance rhythm, your pupil should be aware that the lively character is created not by a lively tempo alone, but by a combination of pace, clarity of articulation and tonal shape.

In music with its own natural momentum, take care to keep the pulse really stable throughout. There should be no hint of rushing, especially when the quavers are shared between the hands in bars 9–15 and 46–52. A few potential danger spots in the quavers, e.g. bars 20–24, might need separate attention, and the end of the first section needs careful pacing.

A mixture of slurred and detached articulation is the most stylish option for the quavers, although they may equally be played legato provided that the finger action is incisive enough to produce a harpsichord-like clarity. Slightly overlapping the left-hand quavers in bar 16 and similar will convey the harmonic progressions, and longer notes may be detached to give a spring to the rhythm.

Trills on the crotchets may be played as three- or four-note mordents (beginning on either the principal or upper note, as appropriate), while grace notes may suffice for the quaver trills, if needed.

Any dynamic decisions are left to the performer. A natural rise and fall in tone is implied by the melodic contours, and stylish echoes can be made when phrases are repeated. In addition, the falling sequences in bars 33–8 suggest a descending 'terracing' of tone before rising to a peak at bar 42. Whatever decisions are made, however (and there are numerous possibilities), the limited tonal range of eighteenth-century instruments must always be observed.

A:5 J. C. F. Bach *Allegro in E minor*

This dance-like piece in the style of a courante is graceful at heart yet contains some daring statements as the hands negotiate some astonishingly wide leaps over the keyboard. Although the editorial phrasing recommends that many of the quavers are detached, the frequent use of arpeggio patterns and broken 6ths makes the piece best suited to a pupil with a comfortable octave span.

Isolating the quavers as they pass continuously between the hands is a useful starting point for developing fluency. Some fingerings may need modifying – for instance, in bar 2 all of the right hand's lower notes may be played by the thumb – but it is important to settle these matters early on. A good sense of keyboard geography is essential for negotiating the leaps in both directions (bars 20–23 are especially treacherous), and memorizing some passages will allow full attention to be given to the hand movements.

Phrasing is a key element in this piece. Slurred and staccato detail should be clearly defined, with care taken to detach the final note of each slur. Confidence will be needed to produce independent phrasing in each hand. Some preliminary staccato training, perhaps using a scale or five-finger exercise, may be necessary in order to develop clarity in the detached quavers. Either a finger or wrist staccato will work, provided that the notes are clearly and lightly separated.

Having considered the minutiae of phrasing it is important to consider the musical whole. The tempo need not be too fast: although there should be a one-in-a-bar feel, the constant quavers create their own busy momentum. The first 'paragraph', ending at the modulation to G major at bar 16, is generally strong in tone, but within the section some gentle dynamic rise and fall will provide variety for the ear. Elsewhere dropping back in tone, as suggested, puts the *forte* into relief and the chance to show the echo in bars 31–2 should not be missed.

A:6 Cimarosa *Larghetto in C minor*

If you are looking for a slow, expressive piece for a musical pupil this is ideal. It has its share of faster notes, especially later on, but textures are simple and the main emphasis is on shapely, musical playing.

Maintaining a consistent pulse can be problematic when the slow tempo and a nervous candidate's heartbeat seem at odds! Although thinking the pulse in four is the only way to keep the phrases flowing, initial subdivision into quaver beats will help gauge relative note-values. Periodic checking with a metronome is also beneficial – and often revealing. Care is needed to keep the hands exactly together in bars 17 and 19, and the rests in bar 11 feel extremely long when given their full value! Practising the extended demisemiquaver groups slowly, and in different rhythms, will help achieve equality of tone and pacing, especially when using the thumb on black notes.

The curvaceous right-hand lines need all the elegance and finesse of the finest wind or string playing (there is a fine arrangement of the movement for oboe and strings). A musical dialogue is created by the alternating *piano* and *forte* in bars 5–8, but otherwise the dynamics act as only the broadest clues as to how to shape the music. Each right-hand fragment needs its own gentle inflection, but the overall shape of each section must also be well thought through – for instance, a slight crescendo through the repeated figures in bar 17 would work well.

Although the main musical interest lies in the right hand, it is equally important to consider the shaping and articulation in the accompanying left hand. The demisemiquavers in bars 17 and 19 are best played smoothly but, elsewhere, detaching some notes would give definition to the bass line; separating the semiquavers in bars 5–8 is particularly effective in evoking bassoon-like articulation. A slackening of pace in the penultimate bar, while observing the marked phrasing, brings the piece to a stylishly poised conclusion.

B:1 Gedike *Miniature in D minor*

This beautiful miniature is very much a song without words. In this case, two voices (soprano and baritone?) seem to be in dialogue and perhaps a third (another treble voice) contributes a passing comment during bars 9–13. The accompanying quavers must therefore be no more than a background presence, their delicate throbbing providing harmony and motion, gently urging the music along. These can be practised initially using a relaxed downward sweep of the hand to develop evenness of repetition. Once this has been mastered, the movement involved can gradually be minimized so that the dynamic is reduced to no more than a murmuring *pianissimo*. The melodic parts, however, need a firm cantabile touch (a singing tone does need some strength), and this will ensure projection and warmth.

A tempo of crotchet = *c.*72 allows for both space and appropriate momentum, although the latter need not be metronomic. The pace at phrase-endings such as in bars 4–5 and 8–9 can be eased a little, but may be increased slightly where greater animation is sensed in bars 11 and 12.

The only marked dynamic is *piano*, so the music should never be played very loudly. However, if the phrases are to have shape and expressive import the hairpins need to be audibly projected, perhaps peaking at a generous *mezzo-piano* in the melodic parts. A more intense sound may also be appropriate between bars 11 and 13, easing off throughout bars 14 and 15. Staccato indications do not imply an unromantically arid texture but merely reflect the slightly detached touch that is in any case unavoidable. The sustaining pedal should be employed throughout, and regular changing on first and third beats will work most of the way through, although, as always, harmonic clarity must be the final arbiter.

This music oozes with romantic appeal, offering plenty of scope for expressive playing – and, for the viewer, the hand-crossing is an added visual bonus!

B:2 Žilinskis *Elegy (In Autumn)*

Autumn's 'mellow fruitfulness' as extolled by English poet John Keats finds its musical counterpart in Žilinskis' warm, sepia-tinted music. To reflect this, the piano tone should be full but not hard, and embedded in a richly pedalled texture.

The right-hand *cantando* often engages finger 1, so sensitive projection rather than poking is required, probably angling the thumb at no more than about 40° to the keyboard. The other fingers, when used melodically, need to be lifted sufficiently to achieve an equivalent depth of sound. Sometimes the left hand contributes melodic fragments (as in bars 14 and 16), which can be played at a very slightly lower sound-level to ensure textural coherence.

Much of the marked dynamic range operates between *mezzo-forte* and *fortissimo*, but this should be viewed in context; while the sound can be rich, it must never be unduly forceful. Offbeat right-hand chords should fulfil an accompanying role, the fingers engaging with the key surface just enough to make the notes speak. The *fortissimo* dynamic needs plenty of supporting bass resonance to avoid an ugly shallowness, and the diminuendo can probably start earlier than marked if the musical deflation from about bar 20 is to be conveyed. The pedal can sometimes be held throughout the bar (as in bars 1 and 2), sometimes changed on the third beat (bars 5 and 7), and sometimes cleared on the fourth beat (bar 8). As ever, listening for harmonic clarity is the best guide.

The motion yielded by crotchet = *c*.69 is suitably elegiac but is also flowing enough for phrases to retain their shape and direction. However, tempo can be flexible, with for example some slight easing at the end of bar 7 and into bar 8. Breathing – metaphorically and possibly literally – between shorter phrase-units (e.g. just before the last beat of bar 2) will also allow the music an appropriate spaciousness.

This piece, when played sympathetically, is richly expressive and is an attractive Grade 5 choice for the romantic temperament.

B:3 Liszt *Andantino*

The virtuosity often associated with Liszt is absent here, yet this miniature packs in a large emotional range. The notes are not hard to play, but the key signature may prove challenging – its E♯ in particular needing to be remembered.

A speed of quaver = *c.*96 seems appropriate for the music's ruminations but, if *espressivo* playing is called for, then flexibility is desirable. Rubato can assist with phrase-shaping in bars 4 and 8, and if the editorial *un poco accel.* is to tell, then the examiner must be made strongly aware of it (without it being inappropriately overstated). Bar 15 to the end can be perceived as a gradual *rit. e dim.* If you agree with the editor's dynamics, then bars 9–14 must be well gauged, leaving something in reserve for the peak at bar 15. It is often a good idea in such cases to leave most of the crescendo until a bar or two before the climax, just hinting at it prior to this. The same is true in reverse for the diminuendo from bar 16, and use of the *una corda* pedal will benefit the last bar.

Texturally, one can envisage an instrumental duo at the opening (possibly two flutes). Fun can be had imagining a suitable orchestration – even trying one out on a sequencing programme – and then mimicking this in terms of piano sound. Pedalling is only marked in three places, but its continual use is essential and changes will need to be quite rapid to avoid blurring. If you are unhappy with the harmonic soup that the scored pedalling produces in bars 14–15, an alternative is to hold the left-hand chord through bar 15, and allow the right-hand chord changes to determine the pedalling.

Liszt often used the key of F♯ major when his thoughts turned heavenwards, so perhaps this is another clue to the character of this poetic miniature.

B:4 Glinka *Mazurka in C minor*

A mazurka is a lively Polish dance but the performance direction for this one is *lamentabile*. 'Melancholy Mazurka' may therefore be a useful concept wherein the right hand sings its heartfelt lament while the left hand provides a reminder of the music's dance origins. Apart from the musical allure of this piece, one attractive practical feature is that bars 9–16 duplicate 1–8, and 21–4 duplicate 17–20, which significantly reduces the learning time.

The tempo should be fast enough for the left hand to generate a gentle momentum but slow enough for the right hand to forge an expressive melodic line, and a tempo in the region of crotchet = 84–92 seems appropriate. The pulse must generally be steady (though not lifelessly rigid), but a gradual ritenuto can be employed effectively in bars 30 and 31.

Textural balance is important and the subdued left-hand part may be played with minimal but relaxed arm movements, gently emphasizing the downbeats. The right hand, though perhaps remaining largely within the confines of *piano* to *mezzo-piano*, can use a more penetrating touch to project over the accompaniment. Glinka marks no dynamics apart from accents and the final *sforzando*, but restraint is sensed. Dynamic nuances can follow the contour of the melodic line and then reflect the thicker texture at bar 25, with a rich but not percussive *forte*. Pedalling is necessary and changing every beat will work, although in places this may need to be adapted. For example, in bar 1 (and later equivalents) the skilful pedaller may wish only to pedal beats 1 and 3, holding the left-hand chord in beat 2 for its full value but allowing a soft staccato note from the right hand. The ensuing right-hand accent may be gently marked through touch, but also through infinitesimal delay.

The piece has its musical challenges but is not technically demanding for this grade. It could also be a useful introduction to the mazurkas of Chopin, whose influence can be detected.

B:5 Schumann *Wiegenliedchen (Cradle Song)*

As with all lullabies, a soothing rocking motion is desirable, generating a befitting sense of solace. However, if the melodic line is not to lose direction, the pace cannot be too slothful; a tempo of crotchet = *c.*92 will work well here. Schumann suggests a ritardando only once but others may be incorporated (in the bars that conclude each half, for instance). Generally the pacing can be flexible, allowing a slight easing of the tempo as one phrase merges seamlessly into the next.

The pedal should be applied through whole or half bars according to the harmony. However, it is useful to practise the music without using the pedal, to check that legato fingering is as efficient as possible. Legato that is achieved entirely through reliance on pedalling is rarely effective whereas legato fingering supported by sensitive pedalling is an ideal combination.

Textural balance is hierarchic, the upper melodic line being the most important, the legato bass line coming next, and the in-filling triplet quavers needing the least projection. For the triplets, the right-hand fingers need to be as still as possible, moving just enough to make the notes sound, while a slightly more positive touch is needed for the outer parts. It may be useful to practise the right-hand technique outside the context of the piece, playing a series of descending or ascending broken triads, holding on to the top note while releasing the lower two. In general, the music operates at levels of *piano* but, to reflect the phrasing, carefully gauged observation of the hairpin dynamic markings can take the sound a little above this. In bars 15–16 and 47–8 it can drop to *pianissimo*, perhaps applying the *una corda* pedal.

This piece should appeal to those of an introspective, sensitive disposition who are happy to lose themselves in an intimate reverie as the baby is lulled gently to sleep.

B:6 Tchaikovsky *Polka*

The performance of nearly all dance music benefits from being felt in and through the body. You can't literally dance at the piano, but your arms and fingers can seem to.

The polka is a lively dance, and a metronome setting of crotchet = *c*.80 will yield a suitable pace – with confidence, it could go a touch faster but not so fast that the dancers are in danger of tripping up! The pulse should be stable, and generally rubato seems inappropriate. The one possible exception is at the end of bar 22 where a hint of easing off – to catch breath! – can add a touch of humour.

The good news for the pedal-shy is that no pedalling is required. However a refined staccato touch is crucial, especially as skilful articulation brings the rhythm to life. Staccato practice may be done outside the context of the piece, perhaps using a three- or four-note pattern and pulling the fingers sharply upwards and inwards after depressing the key. Wrists and forearms should be relaxed but movements must be economical, avoiding splashiness. The acciaccaturas need 'bite' and are best executed by taking the ornament and main note in a single downward motion, briefly catching the acciaccatura as if by accident before sounding the main note. This can initially be practised on a wooden surface where the percussive sound gives a sure indication of articulative clarity.

Marked dynamics range from *piano* to *forte*, though the latter only appears once so the loudest playing should be reserved for bar 22. The hairpin crescendo/diminuendo markings need to be conveyed, and can therefore be practised in an exaggerated way, going from *pianissimo* to *fortissimo* and back. The effect can then be moderated to fit the context. Between bars 9 and 20 the right-hand chords need to be kept light to ensure that the left-hand part is adequately projected.

To obtain more insight into the polka you could trawl the internet for appropriate videos – maybe even take some dancing lessons!

C:1 Thiman *Flood-Time*

If it is excitement that you want from the C List, look no further. Pianists are always delighted to find music that sounds more difficult than it really is, and this skilfully written piece will more than satisfy the pupil who wants to come across like a virtuoso! And in today's world of global warming this is a piece with which we can all identify.

It will be best learnt hands together right from the start, and a useful preliminary method of practice will be to play the broken chords as block chords – it is simply a waste of time looking at every note as a separate entity. With the appearance of the second tune at bar 9, the right hand can be played as minim chords while the attention is given to the left hand. The block-chord practice can continue at bar 17 where the right hand must give extra tone to the dotted-crotchet chords that form a third theme. At bar 37 the first theme returns and sweeps towards a dramatic conclusion.

When it is time to practise the music as written, the aim will be to achieve even quavers that flow seamlessly from hand to hand. In those passages where the left hand crosses over the right, the movement should be continuous without any jerky movements; notice also that the left hand's notes in bars 12 and 16 are high in the treble clef.

Dynamics should be included in the study as early as possible. Too often candidates will blast their way through an exciting piece, forgetting that some of the most dramatic effects are created 'under the breath'. The composer has supplied all the guidance that is needed, both for dynamics and pedalling, and these instructions should not be ignored. For instance, the pedal must remain down for the last four bars if you are to achieve the veritable torrent of sound that concludes this exhilarating piece.

C:2 Gershwin *It ain't necessarily so*

It may come as a surprise to find a piece in Grade 5 that uses the two-against-three binary rhythm in such an exposed way. Many players find it a tricky technique to master, but this may be because they do not meet it until it appears in a complex context that has many other challenges. Here the rhythm is in its simplest form and at a moderate tempo: this makes it easy to hear the halfway point between the second and third notes of the triplet.

The first thing to do is to establish the even flow of the triplets – it may help to recite the words of the title as the notes are played. When that is confident, try tapping straight crotchets on the knee while playing the tune. Teachers have their own ways of introducing this rhythm and as the process of mastering the technique is so important it should not be hurried.

The left hand needs to be practised alone until the jumps are comfortable, and it would be helpful to have fingerings that guide the hand to the correct positions. For instance, in bars 1 and 3 the four bass notes G-D-C-E could use fingers 5-3-4-2. Pedal will usually be changed on the first and third beats of each bar, so the jumps are covered. In the first four bars of the *Allegro giocoso* section, use the second finger to guide the hand into position. The lower note of the second and fourth beats is the same (D♭ in bar 9b, E♭ in bar 10 and A♭ in bars 11 and 12): if the second finger is used on all these notes the jumps will have an anchorage.

Once the notes are mastered it will be easier to think of it as two beats in a bar rather than four, and this will further enhance the laid-back, relaxed atmosphere of the piece.

C:3 Bloch *Joyous March*

Ernest Bloch evidently had a wry sense of humour. The alternating of bars of four beats and bars of three makes an improbable march – unless you are a Disney character who has that odd skipping movement every few steps! In fact, that might be an amusing picture to have in mind while playing.

Slow practice is advised until the unexpected accents and rhythm are firmly fixed in the muscular memory. Look out for the two places where consecutive bars of four beats occur: the first is between bars 17–18 where an extra bar is inserted before the normal pattern is resumed; the second occurs towards the end (bars 48–50) where there are three four-beat bars in a row. Notice also the crotchet rest at the end of bar 49 – it could easily be overlooked.

The touch is predominantly staccato, but this poses no real problem as the tempo (crotchet = 132) is not unduly fast. Allow the arms to drop on the accented chord and then float up with the next one to complete the slur. Although not required, some players might like to add a touch of pedal to these accents. There is a change of mood and tempo at bar 22 where the left hand underpins the theme with a sustained drone-like figure. However, the trickiest passage occurs at bar 42 when the first theme returns, accompanied by persistent quavers. This is rather like patting your head while rubbing your tummy: it will take patience and skill to be able to combine the conflicting articulations without one disturbing the other.

The marchers eventually disappear into the distance but the composer has one more joke up his sleeve, in the form of a loud chord like a cymbal clash at the end. This is not a piece for the faint-hearted, but once safely in the fingers it could be a lot of fun to play.

C:4 Mike Cornick *First Impression*

Pieces by Mike Cornick are always popular, and this gently swinging number will not disappoint. What is the first impression of the title? Players and listeners alike will form their own ideas.

The overriding movement is in triplets (swinging quavers), and the composer tells us that pairs of quavers should be played as crotchet + quaver in triplet time, even if the first quaver is actually a rest. The first phrase, therefore, should sound as though it begins with four matching quavers in triplet rhythm. Examiners notice that candidates often play a straight quaver when it stands alone instead of continuing the triplet movement. There may also be a temptation to play too early the accented chord that appears at the end of some phrases (such as in bars 2 and 4). However, once these details are sorted out, the player will really begin to enjoy the freedom that swing promotes.

Accents, particularly ones that are offbeat, play an important role in the style, so do not be afraid to mark these positively. In this piece several of the final notes or chords of phrases are short and want to be quite abrupt in character so that the following rest makes an impact. Phrases in Classical music usually make a crescendo towards the middle of a phrase and then subside in an arc-like shape. Here most phrases begin fairly quietly and make a crescendo towards their concluding chords. To round off the first and last sections (bars 8 and 25), however, a short tailpiece is added like a quiet aside or unspoken afterthought. Ideally the very last note should be held until it fades away; on no account should it be cut short.

Almost everyone will enjoy this piece, but it would be particularly suited to a pupil who is a little anxious or tense, for it exudes an atmosphere of nonchalance and relaxation.

C:5 Mompou *Pájaro triste (Sad Bird)*

Composers through the centuries have been fascinated by birdsong and many have written music based on the melodies and patterns of different species.

The atmosphere of this lovely piece is created by the use of a repetitive three-note motif, which creates an almost hypnotic effect on the listener, and on the sonorous bell-like chords that underpin it. It is interesting to note that the Catalonian-born Mompou worked for a while in a bell foundry, an experience that profoundly influenced his compositions.

Pedal will be needed throughout, and the curved lines extending from some chords indicate that they should be sustained for longer than their written note-values. The following suggestion for pedalling is just one possible solution. Begin with the pedal already depressed (a special effect that works with a quiet, mysterious start such as this). After that, change the pedal on the first beat of bar 1, the first and second beats of bar 2, the first of bar 3, first and third of bar 4, and so on. A folk melody emerges at the upbeat into bar 8. At bars 9 and 10 the pedal must be changed with every chord until the longer pedals can resume. Where a bass note or chord is tied through two bars (e.g. in bars 12–13 and 17–18), it must be fully sustained by pedal. This will enhance the haunting sound of the distant birdcalls above. Encourage your pupil to experiment and listen to different mixes and sonorities.

Tempo rubato is indicated by the use of *accel.* and *rit.* in two passages, but also by the unusual placing of tenuto lines over the slurs of the opening phrase and elsewhere. These expressive devices should be observed but carefully controlled so as not to distort the shape of the phrase.

If your pupil has imagination and has developed the skill of listening, the beautiful sound-world of this 'Sad Bird' is sure to sing out.

C:6 Christopher Norton *Dreaming On*

There is a mood of contentment and sense of well-being in this rock prelude, but do not be deceived by the apparent simplicity of the notes. The composer marks the piece 'Dreamily' but gives a metronome mark of crotchet = 112, which is quite a challenge. The tempo may be achieved, but without being relaxed and really comfortable under the hands the piece is unlikely to sound dreamy.

Slow practice is essential, with special attention given to the rhythm. The quavers should be straight, not swung, for this style. It would be advisable to begin by becoming familiar with the right hand of the first phrase or two. Once the first twelve bars are secure, almost all the different rhythmic patterns will have been covered, making progress easier for the rest of the piece. Tapping a steady crotchet beat with the left hand or foot while playing the melody will be a useful practice strategy.

When the right hand feels safe, turn attention to the left hand and pedal. A regular pattern of legato pedalling with changes on the first beat of every bar is all that is required, except if there is a definite change of harmony (e.g. in bars 12 and 19). The apparent mixing of sounds that occurs in places like bar 5 or bar 13 is part of the harmonic language. However, bars 11 and 28 contain an important rest that must be heard, so release the pedal with the fourth chord and depress it again on the next. This is a significant moment as the new chord (tied over the bar-line to a minim) is not only syncopated but heralds a change of key, and the direct pedal attack helps to give it prominence. In bar 4 the symbol by the chord simply means that it should be arpeggiated downwards.

As the performance gains in confidence and speed, a feeling of two-in-a-bar rather than four will create a more relaxed flow.

GRADE 6

The challenge of Grade 5 Theory, Practical Musicianship or Grade 5 Jazz will be successfully over as work begins on Grade 6. The slightly different criteria for the higher grades, printed in *These Music Exams*, emphasize the need for the musical character, style and details to come across with conviction. Hopefully, by now your pupil's technical fluency will support these developing ideas, allowing more focus on expressive stylistic aspects.

A:1 Alcock *Almand*

This spirited dance will make a popular choice for those with nimble fingers. Although most of the semiquaver runs are played by the right hand, sometimes the spotlight falls on the left – and these semiquavers must match and sound just as agile.

The few ornaments that appear are important to the style and should not be omitted unless they really cannot be mastered. Higher marks will be achieved if they are successfully included; conversely, a performance with stumbles or delays to the pulse because of the ornaments will lose marks. Only two types of ornament are employed here, and neither is difficult to execute. The first is the short trill that appears at cadences (e.g. bars 2 and 6) and a suggestion for performance is given above the relevant note in the score. The other is a less commonly seen ornament that is played like the familiar Baroque mordent (e.g. bars 3 and 4). This creates an accent on the notes ('mordent' literally means 'biting') and at these moments care must be taken not to upset the even flow of the left hand. If they prove troublesome in the initial stages of learning, try practising without them until the left hand is fluent and the co-ordination confident. Adding them later should be less of a problem.

In common with most keyboard music of this period, no dynamic marks are given, but it is important to add some variety when playing on the blander-sounding modern piano. It was usual to begin a lively piece *forte*. There are possibilities for echo effects (bars 4–5 and 8–9) and also terrace dynamics (or crescendo and diminuendo if preferred) for sequences and passages that ascend or descend. Encourage your pupils to make some suggestions: they are more likely to remember their own ideas in performance. Quavers sound effective if lightly detached, especially those that are upbeats (such as those before the crotchets with mordents).

The almand is not a fast dance and the recommended metronome speed (crotchet = c.76) gives a pleasantly flowing tempo, while a slight ritenuto in the last bar is all that is needed to mark the ending.

A:2 Galuppi *Adagio*

Imagining the sound of a string trio consisting of violin, viola and cello will help to create the right sort of balance and articulation for this serene and beautiful Adagio.

The cantilena-style melody will require a warm singing tone and, for the most part, a legato touch. However, upbeat quavers may be slightly detached (e.g. the final notes of bars 1, 3 and 6), as could the pairs of quavers (as in bars 1, 4 and 5). Dynamics should not be too extreme, but simply rise and fall gently between *mezzo-piano* and *mezzo-forte*, following the shape of the melody.

The viola and cello voices have two distinct roles to play. In the opening bars (and similar) they provide flowing counter-melodies; the viola part, with its offbeat entry and tied notes, needs just a little more prominence than the cello. A good practice strategy would be to rehearse just two voices at a time, swapping the combinations around until each line is satisfactorily balanced with the other. Their second role is to support discreetly with a simple repeated quaver accompaniment that begins in bar 3. These quavers should also be slightly detached as though playing with the typical split-slur bowing technique of string players. If the stretch for the left hand in the second half of bar 6 proves troublesome, take just the demisemiquaver D♯ with the right-hand thumb, lightly touching the key as though it were staccato. The same trick can be used for the G♯ in bar 12.

Ornaments in this piece are really part of the melody, so play them in a smooth, relaxed manner. All the trills begin on their upper notes and, if preferred, the first trill could be reduced to only eight demisemiquavers. Shape the appoggiaturas in bars 4, 5 and 6 by leaning on the first note and resolving quietly on the second.

Rests that occur at the end of a section are often omitted by nervous candidates in exams, so it is advisable to remind your pupils to count carefully, especially when practising at home. That precious silence is part of the atmosphere of the music.

A:3 Handel *Allegro*

The flowing lines and beautiful harmony of this piece, written by a master of the keyboard, make it an appealing choice. As a bonus, the way in which the groups of notes pass from hand to hand encourages graceful, relaxed movements, making the piece ideal as an opener for a recital or exam.

In order to produce a shapely legato line for the melody, listen closely to the way the tied crotchets fade, and, beginning the next note at this level, make a crescendo gently towards the next tied note. Below the melody the accompanying notes should fall away quietly. In bars 3 to 5 there is a very special harmonic progression that tugs at the heart-strings. Using a cycle of 5ths, the bass drops from B to E, A to D and G to C, and the chord sequence begins with the key's minor triads, chords iii, vi and ii, continuing through V, I and IV – a passage to relish. In these bars the first chord will feel stronger than the second, so use the three upbeat semiquavers to make a crescendo towards the stronger chord and a diminuendo towards the weaker.

The most expressive touch used has been legato to this point, but with the appearance of the rows of quavers (briefly over bars 5 to 6, but more continuously from the last beat of bar 8) a lightly detached touch will add some buoyancy to this more extrovert passage. The final chord of each section could be arpeggiated, as a little reminder of the music's harpsichord origin.

The second half has no new technical features, but continues to delight with its harmonic adventures. One uplifting moment is when the bass begins to rise chromatically (bars 25 and 26) until it reaches the reprise of the opening theme, now back in the home key. Dynamics are left to the performer, but the music's genial mood and the style of the period would suggest that they should not be too extreme. Employ subtle shades and nuances to colour the interpretation.

The suggested metronome speed (crotchet = *c*.84) may feel a little quick to some, and a tempo a few notches lower will be perfectly acceptable.

A:4 J. S. Bach *Prelude in D*

The collections of pieces that Bach either wrote or assembled for the musical training of his children are an indispensable part of the repertoire for the aspiring pianist. However, Father was a demanding tutor, and this prelude has a number of technical challenges as well as rich rewards.

After a preliminary play-through, it is a good idea to tackle some of the more challenging passages first. Much of the texture is three-part counterpoint with just an occasional thickening of the harmony (such as in bars 4–5). However, the last five bars fill out into four independent voices, creating some problems for fingerings and note distribution. A few of the notes placed in the upper stave are best taken by the left hand (including the tenor voice's crotchet B at the start of bar 14). In the last two bars, the right hand will have to assist with the lower-stave notes, so that the pedal D can be held. Most editions give help with these decisions, but some adaptation may be needed to suit individual hands. Once this last passage is confident, the rest of the prelude will seem comparatively simple.

Articulation is an important means of expression in Baroque music; it gives a performance greater clarity and character when different types are employed. For instance, all crotchets and tied notes should be legato, while upbeat quavers (as in bar 2) and those in pairs (bar 4) could be detached. Conversely, quavers that move stepwise in a more melodic shape (e.g. in bars 5 and 6) sound effective played smoothly. The semi-quavers could be either legato or played with fingers that attack from just above key level, creating a crisply articulated sound.

Dynamics are a matter of individual choice, but the player must be aware of imitation and the shape of the various motifs. In the rising sequence from bar 8 it would be hard to resist building a crescendo, and that would lead effectively to a triumphant restatement of the first theme deep in the bass (bar 10). The sustained pedal notes (from bar 15) will fade naturally, so a very gradual diminuendo could lead to a peaceful conclusion.

A:5 Cimarosa *Allegro in G*

Domenico Cimarosa was a fashionable composer of the eighteenth century, renowned for his operas. However, in 1924 some 80 single-movement keyboard sonatas were discovered in Florence, apparently written by Cimarosa. Like Domenico Scarlatti's sonatas, they were later grouped into sets of two or three to make more substantial works for performance.

This particular sonata is an attractive, light-hearted piece that will appeal to the pupil with agile fingers and an ear for balance. The right hand has almost all the fun, and it is essential that the supporting left hand is kept light and buoyant. The movement is in a simple sonata form. The first subject closes in bar 8 and a three-bar link introduces the second subject, a group of three short themes in the dominant key. The exposition is concluded with a measured tune in unison quavers and after a brief episode in the minor key there is a full recapitulation.

One of the most common weaknesses heard in the exam room is the over-emphasis of first beats – something to guard against in this piece, with its repeated notes in the left hand. The first theme is made up of four two-bar phrases: shape the first two phrases with a slight crescendo towards the middle (i.e., to the first beats of bars 2 and 4) followed by a diminuendo; if you treat bars 5–8 as a four-bar phrase, with a crescendo towards the beginning of bar 7, this will help the music to flow more expressively towards the cadence.

Regard the demisemiquavers in the first and third themes of the second subject as ornaments. They should be rapid and light without holding back the beat, and only the groups of four (as in bar 28) might cause difficulty. If the given fingering seems fussy, try using the same finger (either a 3 or a 4) on both the second and the fourth notes of the figure, but place finger 2 on the first note of the following group of semiquavers.

The tempo is lively, but beware of starting too fast; think first of the theme at bar 12. A metronome speed of dotted crotchet = 52–6 will give sufficient movement without danger.

A:6 Zipoli *Corrente (Allegro)*

Compared with that of Scarlatti, Zipoli's contribution to the keyboard repertoire is very small, but it contains some real gems. One such is this corrente from the Suite in B minor. It is a piece that entices you to play it over and over again, a virtue to gladden the heart of any teacher!

Give the right hand clearly articulated semiquavers and nuances that follow the rise and fall of the phrasing. The end of each section (bars 30 and 69) could be marked by slurring the first two notes, playing the next two staccato, and then resting briefly on the final quaver. Left-hand quavers should be detached to give a light momentum to the dance, although at cadence points (e.g. bars 22 and 29) a slur on the first two quavers would be attractive. In bars 16–21 the left hand's two voices need to be carefully sustained, with a little more tone given to the tenor line with its tied notes. Be careful of the right-hand passage in bars 23–5: the middle bar has the same notes but in a different order. The same thing happens towards the end of the second half.

It is stylistic to place trills at cadences and these should all begin on the upper note. In bar 22, for example, a triplet of demisemiquavers (using fingering 3-2-3) on the second beat followed by a semiquaver tied to another semiquaver would replace the dotted quaver. The last note of the bar will be as written, and played by the thumb if it is lower (e.g. bar 22) and by finger 3 if higher (bar 29).

As this is harpsichord music no dynamic marks are given, but on the piano some contrasts are really necessary to create musical interest and help shape the phrasing. In general, lively pieces would begin *forte*, and probably end that way too, but beyond that it is up to the individual player to decide. Instead of slowing down at the end of the first section, a slight marking of bar 30 would be appropriate; save a full ritardando for the very last two bars of the piece to make a positive ending. A metronome speed of dotted crotchet = *c*.52 will suit this vivacious dance.

B:1 Chaminade *Élégie*

This is an exquisite yet deeply sorrowful piece from one of the few women composers represented in this piano syllabus. From the first gloomy bottom D the melancholy mood is set: the melody sings its mournful song with just a brief moment of optimism – a golden memory perhaps – in the middle. Throughout it requires subtle nuance, awareness of balance and tonal control, demanding a musically instinctive response from the student.

The left hand must always accompany the melody, relaxing and moving forward to reflect the rubato and expressive rhythmic pliancy needed in the right hand – it should never dictate the pulse. The melody therefore needs to be practised separately (or as a duet with the teacher), perhaps using words to help decide just where to take time, place a note or how to shade the phrases dynamically. Only once such musical intentions are instinctive should the left hand be added.

A sensitive balance between the hands will be crucial. In order to avoid an overly articulate series of semiquavers in the left hand the keys need to be caressed, with the fingers barely allowing the notes to lift to the top of the action. Even within the right hand the lower notes must be kept unobtrusive and light. Avoid misinterpreting the accents, which have no percussive or rhythmic purpose but indicate expressive intent, as if taking a short breath before the note. Good pedalling is also essential; for the most part it should be changed at each shift of harmony and after the bass note so that the root of the harmony is in place. Holding and overlapping the semiquavers with the fingers will give more flexibility and time to do this, avoiding the danger of the intrusive noise that a snatched pedal movement can produce.

The middle section, being almost dance-like in character, could move on a little. And as the notes rise during the improvisatory link back to the opening section there could be a further slight increase in pace – before a gentle ritardando and decrescendo. On no account should this passage sound like a succession of scales but instead the most sensitive of sung melodies.

The *dolcissimo* return of the opening needs to have a captivating and subtle change of colour; using the *una corda* can enhance this. Consider starting the *poco rit.* a little earlier than marked to draw out the tearful ending.

B:2 Grieg *Allegro moderato*

This piece is delightfully attractive and optimistic, full of fantasy and storytelling. It shares the character of incidental music, so will suit the musically imaginative and those who respond well to images.

Technically, however, challenges abound, both in terms of co-ordination and dexterity. Phrasing, note-lengths, pedal, balance and articulation are all inextricably linked; if a casual approach is taken towards any of these elements the piece will not work effectively. The middle chords at the opening, for instance, must be extremely light; the melody should be well projected with just a little more tonal support in the bass notes; the pedal needs to rise at the end of the bar to show the phrasing. The left hand's minims and crotchets must be held with the fingers to maintain harmonic support, particularly in bar 3 where the pedal follows the right-hand phrasing. Here, omit pedal for the first quaver but put it down for the second (the left-hand F held with the finger), then up on the third quaver – this will provide a legato bass line with clearly defined phrasing in the melody. Similar care is needed to hold all relevant notes with fingers in bars 8, 11, 12 and similar. If the phrasing is distinctly articulated the accents need no extra impetus.

In bars 9, 10 and similar some 'shadow' practice may be required to ensure that the left hand moves quickly, grace notes played just before the beat.

The tempo suggested for the opening is slightly conservative; the outer sections will link better to the Vivo if given more of a two-in-a-bar feel. That said, some rubato is appropriate and helpful (e.g. in bars 8 and 12).

Your pupil may find the middle section quite a challenge to manage the articulation and phrasing with the faster tempo. While this section can work without pedal it could benefit from small touches to enhance the phrasing and warm the sound, for example in bars 21, 25, 28. In general, keep the overall touch very light and simple until the crescendo, and make the right-hand quavers staccato to match the left-hand articulation.

This piece sounds wonderful when the performance has fluidity and ease. Playing from memory with the music will enable a musical freedom and inventiveness to be communicated right through to the charming end.

B:3 Nielsen *Mignon*

There is a wonderful story encapsulated in this piece. Whether it is inspired by Goethe's novel or the opera by Ambroise Thomas, it seems to convey Mignon's sad, enforced dance for the gypsies both in the evocative, mournful opening and in the angrier, bullying sections as Mignon is commanded to continue.

There is little to trouble the performer technically in the opening section, and the notes fall comfortably under the fingers in the unusual key of E♭ minor. It needs only sensitivity to balance and a delicate, musical shading of the melody to convey elegance and poetically sweeping movements. Avoid pedal in bars 3, 4 and similar but small dabs will enhance the tone if used sparingly. The grace notes need to be gentle (not snatched); the bass notes require a little more tone than the chords; at the end of bar 4 the phrase should be lifted gently.

The more tricky *Più mosso* requires a well-projected and resolute tenor line right from the end of bar 8, with a fluent yet unobtrusive right-hand accompaniment. Avoid getting too carried away with the *fortissimo* here, as balance is crucial to the clarity of line. Little pedal is needed but as a consequence the bottom E♭ must be held with the finger throughout until it needs to be replayed. In bar 11 the beginning of the second phrase should be clearly defined. The diminuendo and rallentando must be carefully judged to enable a smooth transition into the repeat of the opening.

The ending must come as a surprise and be totally fearless. Slow practice, beginning with a real *piano* and growing quickly to a dramatic and grumpy *fortissimo* (yet with quick movements to cover the final two chords), will help the confidence. Chords should be voiced towards the top to balance the sound.

Once carefully rehearsed, the final bars need to be executed with flair, perhaps anger, and certainly a flourish, as the gypsy shouts his commands at the forlorn young girl. In performance don't forget the final pause: keep the hands poised over where they finish for added dramatic effect, before the musical tension is released and the spell broken.

B:4 Howard Blake *Prelude (Andantino)*

This attractive, very English piece from the composer of *The Snowman* will appeal to young and old alike. The sad, song-like opening is contrasted effectively with a jolly country dance. It is not easy, though, as there are co-ordination and rhythmic issues as well as some awkward left-hand stretches.

The beauty of the opening three lines will only be conveyed if all harmonies are properly supported by the pedal, the balance carefully considered, and the melody sensitively shaped with a little rhythmic nuance. In bar 2 (also bars 4, 10 etc.) the right hand's melody note should be clearly voiced, with the underneath parts gently out of the way. Catching the root notes of harmonies with the pedal is crucial. To achieve this, hold the left-hand bottom Bs with the finger as long as possible and allow the pedal to change slowly. With the quicker pedal changes of bars 5 to 7 bass notes will again need to be held with the fifth finger longer than written in order to avoid a snatched, empty change. Achieving a voiced and focused tone at the top of the octave melody in bar 13 will prevent too heavy and clumpy a sound.

The middle section, moving on a little, needs a lightness of touch to convey the dance feel. Legato pedal is not required; instead, allow some daylight between each dotted-crotchet beat. This should lead to a bright accent on the top B (too much attention to this accent will spoil rather than enhance the character). Bars 27, 28, 31 and 32 should be separated slightly at the bar-line and the pedal in the final three bars of this section changed on the bass notes, providing that the bottom thumb right-hand notes are held as marked.

Don't forget the da capo, using the opportunity of the repetition to explore something even more subtle and sensitive in the sound-world.

B:5 Grovlez *Petites litanies de Jésus*

This gem of a piece – essentially a prayer – is quite beautiful, and will suit a musical, sensitive pianist. The music can be seen as following an imaginary liturgical text, and shouldn't be too rigorously rhythmic. The hymn-like quality of the opening needs space and a chorale character, the top line delicately voiced with a beguiling musical shape. The pedal changes gently on each shift of harmony.

The more legato the top line, the more flexibility the performer will have with the pedal, so the first consideration should be the fingering; this will involve some substitution but will be worth the effort. With the fingering in place, tonal control will follow.

Shading the ends of lines by giving them plenty of time (as if in a resonant church acoustic) is essential; an example is at the end of the first two-bar phrase with its evocative suspension that delays the resolution just a fraction, coaxing the softest of sound. The semiquavers (bars 4 and 32) must have a vocal breadth and be musically shaped – do not hurry the crotchet that follows each figure.

From bar 7 the piece becomes more of a chant, needing breaths at the ends of phrases. Sensitive rubato will add to the meditative ambience, with the most beautiful sound possible for the *pianissimo* moments (bars 10 and 27), perhaps with occasional use of the *una corda* pedal.

The constant rhythmic changes from triplets to duplets, and crotchets to semiquavers, need to be approached without a hint of impatience, sounding naturally pliant. The *plus accentué* should be interpreted as a more passionate declamation of faith, nothing too forceful. In the approach to bar 26 a full, rich and joyous tone is needed; the B♭ left-hand octave should be played just before the beat, and the right hand's preceding octave on E♭ (last quaver of bar 25) held on while the pedal catches the grace note, thereby linking the melodic line to the chord that follows. The *pianissimo* bar after this should be entrancingly evocative before the opening chant returns.

A beautiful sound, tone quality, good balance and an unfailing sense of line and poetry are all needed to do justice to this wonderful piece, but for a student who will respond to these challenges it is the most perfect choice.

B:6 Tchaikovsky *The Witch (Baba Yaga)*

The energy, cackling laughter and occasional ugliness in this piece together paint a vivid picture of the witch of Slavic folklore whose home is a hut standing on chicken legs. Mentioning the threat that she captures and possibly eats children might inspire more practice than usual but may not be necessary, as the piece itself is so acutely pictorial and exciting.

The running, chasing opening with its 'gotcha' chords needs a threaten-ing, scary and light *piano* staccato with a sudden, bright *sforzando*. The technique for this is very specific: a light bounce at the wrist onto well-supported fingers, which actively play the note at the bed of the key. As a little exercise, gently place the third finger of the left hand over the thumb and, placing the end of the third finger and the thumb's final section on a white key, bounce at the wrist. This gives the mechanism, which is then joined by an impetus from the finger to create the shortest staccato. Practise this until it is sufficiently fluent for an exciting tempo to be maintained: dotted crotchet = *c*.100 will work well.

The staccato quavers – the upbeat – are followed by a relaxed, positive drop into the chord, which should be well balanced to the top. Even within these opening bars it is important not to lose sight of the overall phrase; each *sforzando* should become more insistent to bar 4 before dying away a little.

The trickiest passage is perhaps bars 9–12, which need both careful co-ordination and a conversational approach. Avoid being too fussy about the phrasing in the left hand, as the joining of the final two quavers is not absolutely essential or significant. Bars 12 to 24 require a sense of quiet urgency: the chords, if kept suitably short, will by their nature provide a horse-like (or chicken-like) rhythmic energy as the witch's house runs in pursuit of the unfortunate victim, finally screaming in frustration in bar 27 before running into the distance. The decrescendo needs careful grada-tion, fading to nothing in the final bars, so in bar 40 the *pianissimo* should not be too quiet, allowing the witch and house to run away over the horizon.

C:1 S. C. Foster *Soirée Polka*

Although best known as a composer of songs, Stephen Foster wrote a small body of piano music of which this attractive polka is a good example. The notes all lie comfortably under the fingers, but a light, dancing style of execution is called for if the polka character is to be conveyed.

It is inappropriate to play the music too speedily although the suggested metronome mark of crotchet = *c*.100 could be raised to 108 for the more confident player. Fingerwork should sparkle, especially the semiquaver triplets which need to be clearly articulated, with a strong sense of the finger coming out of the key after striking. The left-hand leaps in places such as bars 1–7 will require careful practice. One strategy is to memorize the music for a few bars so that the hand's positions on the keyboard can be visually located – but do be sure that your pupil knows where on the page to look back! Another strategy is to memorize kinaesthetically, slowly building up the speed of the arm motion while looking away from the keyboard, so that the motion itself becomes habitual.

Much of the articulation, especially in the left hand, involves a light staccato. There are times, however, when left-hand outer fingers need to sustain the notes in order to bring out either a prominent, rhythmically supportive bass line (e.g. bars 9–15) or a brief counter-melody (e.g. bars 27–8). At such points the inner fingers of the left hand should be kept relaxed and free to facilitate a more detached articulation on the upper notes. A little pedalling can be included, mainly to add slightly extra weight to downbeats such as in bars 1, 3 and 17.

The three marked dynamic levels should be clearly differentiated. However, more subtle nuances may be incorporated to outline the sense of a two-bar phrase at, for example, bars 17–18 and 19–20, where the former of these starts more strongly than it ends and the latter slightly rises to and away from bar 20.

This charming period piece, if stylishly played, will bring a Grade 6 programme to a spirited close.

C:2 Rodrigo *Pastoral*

Rodrigo was a highly skilled pianist who composed regularly and idiomatically for his instrument. This piece evokes an idyllic pastoral landscape, which will suit sensitive players.

The piece is in A–B–A form, but when the 'A' material returns at the end of bar 44 it is enriched and elaborated. In this section, care with balance is needed to ensure that upper melodic parts receive sufficient arm-weight for the melody to sing out effectively. The right-hand quaver (immediately after the downbeats in bars 53–63) must be played especially gently, as it is part of the accompaniment. To reflect the different mood and colour of the passages it may help to imagine a flute playing the melody during the earlier sections of the piece and then an oboe taking the lead from the return of the 'A' section at the end of bar 44.

Although a fairly broad dynamic range is marked, the sound should never be forced – it may be helpful to think of *forte* as signifying 'full' rather than 'loud'. At the opposite end, *una corda* can be engaged to aid the ethereal *pianissimo* sound-world in bars 58–66. Left-hand 'cuckoo' figures need slight projection with a gently detached touch, whereas similar figures in the right hand, at a higher dynamic level and in the treble register, can largely be left to speak for themselves. In bar 43, the leap from the treble G to the lower B needs to be done unhurriedly (within the context of a ritenuto) so as to avoid a bump.

A restful flow at dotted minim = *c*.50 underpins the atmosphere, but there can be flexibility. In addition to marked tempo modifications, there should be no sense of hurrying from one phrase to the next, as if allowing time to breathe. However, phrases should be played legato and connect with each other, so pedalling the third beat of each bar will help. In bars 45–6 and 49–50 the bass notes need to be sustained, and to avoid harmonic blurring, the adept foot can half-pedal at bars 46 and 50 – alternatively the foot can be lifted slowly during the space of the same bars.

Above all, musical imagination, via the fingers, should be used to convey an audio portrait of rural calm and charm.

C:3 Takemitsu *Clouds*

The title of this atmospheric piece offers a clue to its performance. The music seems to drift past with no awkward angles or abrupt switches, just a gentle morphing from one state to the next.

Takemitsu suggests a broad tempo range, so it is a safe bet to opt for somewhere in the middle, perhaps crotchet = *c*.54. The melodic parts need to sing out, untroubled by the thicker accompanying chordal textures. In the more awkward left-hand passages (such as bars 9–12 and 29–32) take every opportunity to relax when lifting upwards from the keyboard, keeping the physical motions as free and calm as possible. To this end, it may also be helpful to play the E at the beginning of bar 5 with the left hand, because only big hands will be able to cope comfortably with the notated layout.

The score includes quite a wide dynamic range. The *forte* can be lyrical, using a firm, deep touch for intensity and never hitting the keyboard. Subtlety is required to achieve the crescendos and diminuendos, but over-projection when practising can be useful. It is easy to imagine that one has executed a subtle crescendo when in reality the effect is inaudible to the listener, so, over-projecting the dynamics before putting them in context may guard against their being ineffective. Where the left hand has the melody (bars 22–8), fingers and wrist can be lifted a little so that the sound is chiselled out, cutting through the right-hand accompaniment which must be particularly subdued. Inner right-hand parts in bars 4 and 5 also need subtle projection, but not so much that the lingering tone of the upper melodic notes is masked.

Pedalling is essential, and most of the way through it is appropriate to change on the beat. In bars 3 and 23, however, the foot can be lifted a little earlier to accommodate the D♯. For an effective staccato in bars 33 and 34, no pedalling is required but the right hand needs a good legato fingering.

The music has its gentle surprises but these are never shocks, and this piece is an attractive introduction to Takemitsu's fascinating sound-world.

C:4 Finney *Jack Rabbit*

The jack rabbit is a type of hare. Its running and bounding motions are skilfully portrayed in this musical character piece which calls for imagination and disciplined fingerwork.

The tempo of crotchet = *c*.112 sets a lively but manageable tempo – although the more dextrous among your pupils could go a little faster. For the longer triplet runs, good fingering is important. For example, in bars 8 and 9, arranging the fingering so that both hands use a thumb on F (bar 8) then on C and the higher F (bar 9) provides some helpful points of synchronization. In other places a less conventional tactic can be applied: in bar 30, for example, the right hand can finger the triplets 1-2-5 and 2-3-5 and then use 3/1 for the A♭/E chord of the next bar. Smooth execution is perfectly possible as long as the arm is kept relaxed and the wrist movements are not jagged.

The music is strongly rhythmic, and realizing this in performance aids the musical picture. The rhythms that occur in the opening bar and subsequently in 12, 17 and similar need to be sharply etched, the semiquaver being played as close to the second beat as possible and the preceding semiquaver rest being distinct. These rhythms should be audibly differentiated from the opposing triplet patterns.

Dynamics need to be contrasted boldly. The *fortissimo* tone, using a swift downward attack, can border on hardness, with a generally dry piano sound in evidence much of the time, even when playing *pianissimo*. Staccatos can be very crisp, the finger being lifted smartly upwards and inwards after the key-release. Pedal use is marked only once. However, a discreet application may help in bars 29 and 30, and at the end of the paused notes (for example in bar 3), so that the sound is sustained while the hands are repositioned.

For the theoretically minded, this piece is a useful introduction to serial technique in that it is based entirely on the six pitches shown at the top of the score. They are often transposed and not always presented in the same order, but fun can be had working out how Finney has stayed within this compositional stricture yet let his imagination roam.

C:5 Frank Martin *Clair de lune (Petit nocturne)*

The title of this piece may lead one to expect a sweetly perfumed miniature along the lines of Debussy's early masterpiece. However, Martin's musical nightscape, written in 1952, is much more eerie and disturbing in character, perhaps evoking the darkness rather than the romance of the night.

Much of the music is in two parts and, in order to achieve a desirable balance between right and left hands, it may be helpful to imagine an oboe and viola duo in which timbres are both contrasting and complementary. The right-hand threnody can be played *cantabile* (as marked) with a deep, firm touch, allowing every note its full value, while the left hand can be held close to the keys, using just enough finger movement to keep the murmuring semiquavers even. It is helpful to position the left hand fairly well forward on the keyboard so that the upper black notes can be reached easily by the thumb.

The metronome mark of quaver = 88 yields a gently flowing tempo, allowing enough motion for the *riten.* and *rall.* markings to be effectively observed. The expressive musical lines have an inbuilt flexibility which can be realized through subtly increasing and decreasing the tempo. For example, in bars 13–17 intensity builds towards the right-hand's B♭♭ and then unwinds, settling eventually on the E♮ at the beginning of bar 17. In terms of dynamics, the first page may be played at a general *piano* level although the rise and fall of the phrases can be reflected through dynamic shading. The second page is more dramatic, including a general crescendo and diminuendo, although the qualifying *un poco* in front of the *forte* at bar 14 should be noted.

Pedalling is necessary if the atmosphere is to be conveyed to the listener. Generally, pedalling each crotchet beat works, although this may need to be modified in places where there are demisemiquaver elaborations. However, really subtle pedalling can only be determined through careful listening.

In a sensitive performance this piece is haunting and evocative – and do enjoy the moment when the light of C major shines through in the final *pianissimo* chord.

C:6 O. Peterson *Jazz Exercise No. 3*

Oscar Peterson's collection of short jazz pieces (from which this exercise is taken) provides an excellent introduction to jazz idioms and techniques. In this piece the composer explores some attractive syncopations and typical jazz harmonies.

The music sounds best when swung, whether the notation is shown as even quavers or as dotted rhythms. The quaver chords in bar 22 are exceptions and may be played straight and in a free tempo. Minim = 63 will give the music a relatively laid-back character, but holding a steady pulse is crucial. There should be no hurrying through syncopations such as in bars 6–8. In the early stages of learning, it may help to play these bars to an audible beat (using, if all else fails, a metronome). For the music to sound natural, however, the pulse must be internalized then expressed in a nonchalant rather than a military manner.

Acquiring a good fingering is, as always, necessary. In bars 17 and 19 the semiquavers can be divided between the hands and, in bar 21, arranging the fingering so that both hands use third fingers on the A and on the E♮ will encourage co-ordination. Pedal can aid the more awkward joins and leaps, such as in bar 2 and especially in bars 14–15. Discreet pedalling may be desirable elsewhere (certainly in the last two bars).

There are no dynamic markings but the examiner is unlikely to appreciate a monochrome performance – usually a musical death-knell whatever the style! An appropriate general level might be *mezzo-piano*, rising slightly at bar 6 before reducing the sound to reflect the descending harmonic sequence in bars 6–8. A similar scheme might be tried in bars 14–16. Vocalizing the quaver patterns ('scatting') can determine some natural emphases that occur moment by moment within a phrase. A similar effect can then be tried by transferring the vocal nuances to the keyboard.

When familiarizing oneself with a musical style there is no substitute for listening. While there are plenty of recordings of Peterson himself, it is also worth hearing Bill Evans. His 1972 recording of *Turn Out the Stars* (from about 0' 41") is a model of style and tone.

GRADE 7

The final grades should be equally rewarding not only to the pupils but to the teachers, parents and mentors whose support and involvement in the exams should be bearing much fruit. The playing usually sounds quite accomplished even at a pass level, while merit and distinction categories will acknowledge musical and polished performances of real artistic quality. The highest marks most frequently go to candidates choosing pieces within their own technical comfort zone, so that expressive details and communication can lift the music off the page.

A:1 T. A. Arne *Allegro*

In this piece, dating from 1756, one can hear how Baroque style is gradually giving way to Classical, especially with regard to form. The music is cast in a simple sonata form, and an understanding of this may be a basis for interpretation since Classical expression is often embedded in form.

The suggested speed of crotchet = *c*.96 offers a comfortable flow – manageable by most players at this grade – and is one which matches Leopold Mozart's definition of *allegro* as 'a lively but not overly fast tempo'. The pulse should be held steadily, although a slight ritenuto may be appropriate in the final bar. As always, adopting a good fingering – such as that suggested in the score – is a prerequisite for fluency, and should be encouraged from the earliest stages of learning. At the end of bar 22 the collision of the right- with the left-hand B may be addressed by taking the note with the left hand then holding it down, thus retaining the sense of harmonic progression. Generally the music demands a clear, precise touch – firm but never forced, contained but never flabby.

Neither articulation nor dynamics are indicated, but the music would sound dull on the modern piano if there were no variety. Articulation may be mixed, with, for example, adjacent quaver pitches forming legato phrases (as in the left hand of bars 1 and 27) and non-adjacent ones receiving a detached execution (as in the left hand of bars 2 and 8). Right-hand semiquavers require clear articulation, each finger being lifted after striking the note to avoid blurring or overlapping. To achieve a convincing dynamic scheme it is important to listen to the musical contours and inherent tension and release in the piece itself. For example, the opening invites *mezzo-piano* with a crescendo in bar 2, reaching *forte* by bar 3. The chordal passage from the end of bar 8 suggests a fuller sound, perhaps less so in the recapitulation at bars 34–6, where a subsequent crescendo to bar 37 can be effectively incorporated, followed by a diminuendo in the last two bars. More localized nuances can also be included, as for example in bars 19 and 20 where a slight crescendo/diminuendo can help to stress the expressive midpoint of the bar. Whatever scheme is devised it must complement and not antagonize the music. Although pedal use is not actually necessary, there are places where it is helpful, such as in bars 3, 8–9 (chords) and later equivalents.

The genial mood of this music and its gentle drama make it an attractive choice for most candidates.

A:2 Handel *Allemande*

Handel's keyboard suites are less well known and less frequently played than those by J. S. Bach, yet this allemande is a musical gem. It does not call for huge finger dexterity but it does require clarity of texture and part-playing.

The serious nature of the music suggests a generally legato approach in which finger substitution will occasionally be necessary to keep the lines smooth. Legato connections between the fourth and fifth finger in the left hand (needed in bars 4–5) is another technique that will have to be mastered. Although the pace of the music is not fast – the editorial suggestion of crotchet = *c*.56 seems appropriate – fingering needs to be given great care, if control of the musical intricacies is to be secure. There is no need to avoid using the pedal as long as its application discreetly aids the preservation of legato and is not a substitute for good fingering!

The nature of the music will also determine any dynamic interest, and the minor key and gentle momentum suggest a basic *piano* level from which the sound may gain in intensity as appropriate. For example, the notational shape from bar 1 to bar 5 describes a shallow arch which can be reflected by a slight crescendo/diminuendo to and from the middle of bar 3. Within the larger phrases there are also points of stress which subtle dynamic emphasis can bring out – the suspensions in bars 12 and 13 provide good examples of this.

Ornamentation is an expressive feature of the keyboard writing that should enhance the melodic line. To this end, and to avoid interruption to the flow, the ornaments should not be played too speedily or with too much attack; they can be approached calmly and must sound natural. If the execution of the ornaments (as indicated by the editor) presents undue difficulties, then simplifying them is an acceptable option but, at this level, they should not be omitted. In some instances (e.g. bar 5) a three-note ornament would be acceptable, as preserving the flow and mood of the music is more important than authenticity.

The pulse must be steady, but a metronomic feeling is best avoided. Within the regularity of the beats and bars there can be some flexibility to allow expressive points to be made. For example, the onset of bar 10 may be fractionally delayed to highlight the interrupted cadence, and phrase-endings (such as in bar 5) may be marked by a hint of ritenuto – which can be a little more pronounced before the double bars.

Technique at the service of expression is certainly called for here.

A:3 Mozart *Presto*

This sprightly sonata movement requires a sense of playfulness as well as nimble, disciplined fingers, but it comes with a twinkle in its eye!

The semiquaver patterns lie comfortably under the fingers but fluency will only be achieved after slow, careful practice – possibly engaging altered rhythms and using a suitable, consistently applied fingering. Technically, the split octaves (bars 90–97) may be new to your pupil and will need careful preparation. The forearm should remain relaxed so that a flexible but contained rotation can take place, allowing thumb and fifth finger a precise, accurately timed articulation. Using finger 4 on the black notes may aid fluency for larger hands. The Alberti figures (for example, in bars 42–6) demand active fingers for clarity, but small, economical movements for balance.

The suggested tempo of dotted crotchet = *c.*72 yields an appropriate momentum but this can happily be raised to *c.*80 for the more agile player. A steady pulse is necessary, and strict counting of rests in bars 2–4 and later equivalents is vital if the humour of the passage is to be conveyed. However, the pauses in bars 37 and 148 need to be significant to have the appropriate impact, and the slightest hint of a ritenuto at the very end can signify closure.

Dynamically the piece thrives on strong contrasts, often switching from *piano* to *forte* or vice-versa, and bringing out these contrasts adds to the character of the music. When practising, it may be useful to exaggerate the dynamic extremes to ensure their projection in performance, albeit in a manner appropriate to the Classical style. However not all of the *forte* markings seem to prescribe mere loudness. For example, in bars 43–8 there is a feeling that the *forte* implies a gentle first-beat emphasis to enhance the musical shape and direction of the passage. In such cases, sensitivity to context is an important criterion for determining a dynamic level.

Articulation is clearly marked in the score or helpfully suggested by the editor but, as Denis Matthews observes, a light texture is desirable in the exposition and recapitulation to throw into relief 'the mock-fiery outbursts in the development' – thus further emphasizing the musical humour. Pedalling is not necessary for much of the piece but it can help with passages in legato 6ths and 3rds, and also enhance connection of repeated notes in places such as bar 38 or, more particularly, bar 50.

Examiners will enjoy performances that are neat and bring out the humorous elements.

A:4 C. P. E. Bach *Allegro*

This sturdy music should appeal to the more extrovert player who has strong fingers and a sense of drama, but who prefers runs in small doses! Crotchet = *c*.84 sets a realistic pace, but the more confident player could raise this to *c*.92. Rubato is generally not necessary, although a small pause for breath between bars 19 and 20, and a very slight ritenuto into bar 39, can help to outline the form of the music – indeed, this concise movement can serve as an introduction to sonata form.

Although the touch can be firm – even a little brusque in the more dramatic parts – it should never be over-weighty or unduly lingering. Sprightly fingertips are needed in the runs commencing at the end of bars 15, 32 and 49, and a systematic fingering will also be essential, in which note repetitions are achieved through rapid finger changes. This is a technique that, if unfamiliar, can first be practised outside the context of the piece.

Bach indicates some basic dynamics in the score, but these can be supplemented by others. For example, the detached notes of the opening bar (and later similar bars) can be played *forte* as well as detached, while the subsequent rising thirds invite a slightly quieter dynamic to complement the legato touch. The strong opening motif briefly reappears in the left-hand part in some unexpected places (bars 10, 38, 44), so it is worth projecting this musical feature through the dynamics. It is also a good idea to observe the *piano* marked in bars 18 and 52 to highlight the unexpected harmony, and the subsequent rest should not be shortened if the full effect of the passage is to be experienced. Use of the pedal is not actually necessary, but it can enrich chordal textures at, for example, the first beats of bars 1 and 2, and the first and third of bar 13.

The music contains a number of different ornaments. For those interested, C. P. E. Bach wrote extensively on the subject of embellishments in his *Essay on the True Art of Playing Keyboard Instruments*, covering those required by this movement. The most important thing to remember is that the ornaments must complement rather than interrupt the musical lines. Bach's words on trilling are worth quoting: 'Trill slowly at first and then more rapidly but always evenly. The muscles must remain relaxed or the trill will bleat or grow ragged. Many try to force it. Never advance the speed of a trill beyond that pace at which it can be played evenly.' Sound advice indeed!

A:5 J. S. Bach *Sinfonia No. 10 in G*

Bach composed his sinfonias primarily for educational reasons: once a student had mastered two-part playing, as found in the two-part inventions, he or she could progress to more advanced three-part work. If this pedagogy sounds very uninspiring, don't worry, for the music itself is anything but! In a skilful performance there is a seamless flow from which emerges the gem-like perfection of Bach's counterpoint.

A tempo range in the region of crotchet = 68–76 yields an appropriate pace, fast enough to create a sense of forward motion but not so fast that articulative clarity is threatened. Generally, the tempo can be held steadily throughout, although some minimal rubato may be applied around cadences, as at bars 21–2 and 25–6, with maybe a slight rallentando in the penultimate bar.

Clarity of texture and evenness of flow will be paramount concerns, thus it is important to determine how the middle voice is to be distributed between the hands. A suitable scheme is indicated in the ABRSM edition, catering for more or less any size of hand, and there are also some helpful fingering suggestions. The benefits of a systematic approach to selecting and practising a good fingering cannot be stressed enough. Articulation should be clear, with no lingering fingers, especially in semiquaver passages. The opening left-hand crotchets and subsequent accompanying quavers in both hands may be played detached (rather than staccato), except where ties in the inner part make this impractical, as in bars 8–9 (right hand) and 16–19 (left hand). However, a legato approach is appropriate for the more melodic right-hand quavers between bars 22 and 25, where phrase shaping is also desirable.

Dynamic nuances may be incorporated to reflect the natural musical contours, but some larger gestures can be considered too. For example, a crescendo in bar 15 anticipates the musical high-spot in bar 16, from where the sound can diminuendo to bar 20. Likewise, a crescendo can be applied from bar 26 to about halfway through bar 27, after which a diminuendo to bar 31 is the natural consequence. You can then choose either to continue reducing the volume towards a quiet ending, or to opt for a grander finish by gradually getting louder from bar 31. Both ways can sound equally convincing in an artistic rendition. Use of pedal is not really necessary, but it may aid the fingers as a joining device at, for example, beats 2 to 3 of bar 21.

Once mastered, this piece is a joy to play and is certainly a gift to the tidy-fingered and tidy-minded musician.

A:6 Daquin *Le coucou (The Cuckoo)*

Although Daquin wrote a substantial body of organ, harpsichord and choral music, it is due to this single piece that his name has become more familiar. Its attractions are obvious as it takes the player on a lively spin, including good-humoured cuckoo effects (in both hands) along the way. However, nimble fingerwork at an appropriate tempo (crotchet = c.112–120) over an extended period are prerequisites for a successful performance.

Remember that the piece is subtitled 'Rondeau' and, in whatever way the rondo sections are presented in your edition, the formal plan of a rondo is A–B–A–C–A, so if any portion is omitted the performance is incomplete. (In the ABRSM edition the B and C sections are referred to as '1er Couplet' and '2e Couplet'. The ABRSM bar-numbering scheme is used in this note.)

For learning purposes, it is a good plan first to master the semiquaver figures in the right hand in bars 1–9 and 43–6, and in the left hand in bars 32–9. Once this is done, the music's most demanding patterns and finger motions will be familiar. The subsequent sequences and figures in different keys will take less time to assimilate as a result. A good fingering, such as that supplied in the ABRSM edition, is essential. To preserve evenness and dexterity in sequences, for example bars 6–9, the finger should be changed on the repeated note and the new hand-position safely established. Slow practice in the early stages of learning will pay dividends.

Played on the piano this music invites a dynamic response. Editorial suggestions in the ABRSM edition make sense: *piano* for the A sections, *mezzo-piano* for the B section and *pianissimo* at the start of the C section with a crescendo to bar 56. It could add yet more interest if a different dynamic level is adopted for the A section on each of its appearances, say *piano, mezzo-piano, mezzo-forte*. The sound, however, should never be strident, so keeping the arms and hands relaxed would also keep the sound relaxed. As the 'cuckoo' figures supply pictorialism but also provide rhythmic impetus they should cut through the texture but without drowning the accompanying semiquavers. An appropriate effect will be produced if the quaver is played staccato and the crotchet slightly marcato. Neither pedalling nor rubato is needed, although a slight ritenuto at the very end will signify conclusion.

Le coucou, once mastered, lies very comfortably under the pianist's fingers and is a pleasure both to play and to listen to.

B:1 Bruch *Schwedischer Tanz in A minor*

Understanding the form of this expressive dance will go a long way towards building a convincing interpretation. There are three themes, and all are subjected to the technique of variation. Once this is realized, the task of successfully balancing the themes and the material that surrounds them becomes much more straightforward.

The first theme is eight bars in length and repeated an octave higher with the texture filled out and some doubling with octaves. The second theme (bar 16) is only four bars long, but is played twice, its repeat embroidered with trills. The third theme (bar 24) acts as a cadential or closing theme that very significantly concludes with a restatement of the last phrase of the first theme. This phrase now assumes the character of a refrain, a common feature in folk music. At this halfway point (double bar), the first theme begins again, now passing from hand to hand in the middle of the texture: three notes in the right, three in the left, and then back again to the right, before settling in the left hand (bars 37–9). At the upbeat into bar 41 the left hand retains the first theme while the right weaves a semiquaver pattern above. The second theme has fewer adventures in this half and the most significant feature of the closing theme is the way its refrain melts on to the major chord (*tierce de Picardie*) at bar 63.

Learning first the notes and then how to control the different layers will probably begin with some separate-hands practice. One of the challenges will be to manage the trills while holding the sustained notes below (bars 21–3). An easy option is to take the tied E crotchets and the D♯ that follows with the left hand. Prepare by using fingers 5, 3 and 2 on the first left-hand chord in bar 21 so that the thumb can play the tied notes; the right hand is then free to shape the melody and trills unimpeded. A seven-note trill beginning on the principal note would be best, but don't be afraid to play just five (in effect a turn). Another vital skill is that of playing melody notes and accompaniment, or in this case fragments of accompaniment, in the same hand. Patience and close listening are required, and, as this texture is commonly found in Romantic music, the technique is worth mastering.

Legato pedalling will be required throughout the piece. It will be necessary to change at every half bar (e.g. the first two bars) or sometimes just on the first beat of a bar (e.g. bars 3 and 4) where there is only one harmony per bar. Pedalling should only stop when a rest must be heard (bars 8 and 16). The *una corda* pedal can be added at the two appearances of the closing theme, which are marked *pianissimo tranquillo*.

With a little extra effort this piece offers a lot of pleasure.

B:2 Skryabin *Prelude in D flat*

Almost all the pieces in Grade 7 List B will require some preliminary study if the composer's intentions are to be understood. This elusive prelude by Skryabin is no exception.

The first thing to notice is the predominantly quiet level of the dynamics, with just a few phrases rising a little above this. Only once does *mezzo-forte* appear and that quickly subsides to *pianissimo*. The *una corda* pedal is indicated at the beginning; it would be quite feasible to keep it on for the entire piece. A wide range of dynamics, more than enough for the piece, is possible even with this pedal depressed.

Everything about the piece is subtle. The given tempo changes indicate only a slight increase in speed from one section to the next. Starting at crotchet = 66, the tempo changes to 69 at bar 9 and increases gradually to 72 at bar 19. The *a tempo* instruction at bar 28 probably means a return to the original speed, but this is open to question. These adjustments to the tempo – along with indications for rubato, accelerando and ritenuto – are almost imperceptible but are part of the intrinsic flexibility of the music.

The piece grows out of a single idea: a fluttering figure that is heard first in three descending groups. If one were to give this piece a title, 'Butterfly' would admirably describe both the movement of the music and the delicacy with which it must be played. The role of the left hand is simply to provide the gentlest of backgrounds. Pedal will be required throughout, and pianists must always be ready to adjust their pedalling according to the piano and the acoustic in which they find themselves playing.

The most challenging passage begins at bar 19 where not only have the notes doubled in speed but the music has reached its fastest tempo. It is a decorated version of the original motif, now spilling down two octaves. A comfortable fingering will be vital and it will be helpful to find one that retains the same pattern for both octaves and which suits all three of the descending groups in bars 19–21. Try using 5-2-4-1-2-3-1 and then, turning the wrist, reach over to continue on the D♭ with 2-5-1-2-3-5. This brings the hand to rest on the first beat of the next bar. The hand should feel very relaxed and soft, the fingers flat as though tickling the keys – like the fluttering of a butterfly's wings.

B:3 Turina *Conchita rêve (Conchita Dreams)*

The comparatively uncomplicated texture and technical requirements of this descriptive piece will make it a popular choice. It will be fun deciding what Conchita is dreaming about; it sounds as though she is having some exciting adventures! The sudden loud outbursts and the unexpected passage of dotted rhythms conjure up the fierceness of the Spanish sun and the colourful dances and music of flamenco with its guitars, castanets and drumming heels. The influence of folk music is everywhere in this piece.

The harmonies are often unusual, so be wary about the accidentals in the learning stage. Much of this could be learnt hands together from the start, just selecting a few more complex passages for separate-hands practice. It will require straightforward legato pedalling, changing with the harmony – but ensure that the rests are heard in bars 2, 16 and 40. The leap from bar 2 into bar 3 (and similar) must not cause a delay, so have the right hand in position before playing the two quavers to allow the eye to be on the left hand. If the stretch in bar 9 (and, for some, bar 10) is a problem, play the two lower notes just before the beat, but be sure to catch these notes with the pedal so that the bass is intact.

Be very precise about the rhythm of the dance-like figure at bars 15 and 16. The double dots should be really crisp and the tempo must not be allowed to slacken to accommodate the quicker notes. If an alternative fingering for the left hand is preferred, try 4/1 on the C#/G# chord and 5/1 on D/A. The other notes are fingered as indicated in the score. There will be a temptation to play this exciting passage loudly, but *pianissimo* still prevails until the *sforzando* in bar 16. It might be helpful to imagine the sound coming from a distance.

As the score indicates, dynamics are an important part of the interpretation, and they should be followed faithfully. At bar 17 the first theme returns, but with some extra notes tacked on. These rising quavers and triplets sound like decorative figures and are best played quieter as though drifting away. The ending is very quiet, and it would be effective to use the *una corda* pedal from bar 33 onwards. There is no need to slow down at the end as the composer has in effect built in a rallentando by using the device of augmentation for the last four notes.

B:4 Granados *Viniendo de la fuente (Coming from the Fountain)*

One can almost feel the warmth of a Spanish evening in this beautiful evocation of a childhood scene. Before the days of piped water, families would carry water home from the local fountain. It is possible that this piece was inspired by a picture of village life, for Granados was not only a composer but also a fine artist who gained much inspiration from paintings.

The first theme, a folk-like melody, sings serenely above a repetitive, flowing left-hand accompaniment that remains firmly rooted in the tonic chord. In between these two layers a counter-melody wends its way. Some preliminary right-hand practice would be advisable, because the only real technical challenge of this piece lies in keeping the lower notes quiet while projecting and shaping the principal melody above. (Watch out for the unexpected Gb that appears in bar 10 and again in bar 39.)

Once the right hand is mastered, there will be no difficulty adding the accompaniment. The left hand should lie close to the keys, the fingers gliding from note to note. If the fifth finger holds down the low Ab, only releasing in time to replay it, the pedal can be changed whenever it seems necessary without losing the sonority and fullness of the texture. These changes may be on every beat, or less frequently as long as the melody is not obscured.

A new tune emerges in the left hand at bar 14, growing out of the previous bar's rising quavers (a little crescendo will help announce its arrival). Notice here that the *pianissimo* indication is for the right hand only; the left hand is marcato. However, the melody shifts back to the right hand with the last three quavers of bar 17, and in bar 21 a *rall.* heralds the return of the first theme. Take time over bar 21, especially lingering over the crotchet C, as this is the first note of the melody but still within the rallentando.

The material is now repeated to make a simple A–B–A–B–A structure, so there are only 21 bars of notes to learn – a bonus for those with a busy schedule! With the last appearance of the main theme (at the upbeat into bar 36), try using the *una corda* pedal for a change of colour. The music is gradually dying away, as though the children are disappearing into the distance or slipping back into the past.

B:5 Liszt *Romance in E minor*

Liszt's beautiful transcription of his own song 'O pourquoi donc' will appeal to pianists who enjoy a challenge and love Romantic music. They will also need patience in order to establish a secure left hand. The flowing accompaniment, reminiscent of a Chopin nocturne, is divided between the hands at first, but then requires the left hand to range widely across the keyboard.

In tackling the first 'verse' it would be helpful to practise the accompaniment alone, letting the notes flow seamlessly from hand to hand. Once this is comfortable and the notes familiar, add the melody. It will need a warm singing tone while keeping the rippling accompaniment subdued. With the second 'verse' (at bar 40) the accompaniment, now solely in the left hand, flows in triplets and the mood becomes agitated. The accompaniment consists of two main patterns. The first has a repeated note halfway through the bar where a change of finger is advised. In bar 40, for instance, left-hand fingering could be 5-2-1-2 and 4-2-1-2-4. The second is a simple arpeggio figure: here, it would be a good idea to cover the notes in just two hand-positions rather than turning the hand over the thumb in the conventional way. This technique evolved during the Romantic period when pedalling allowed greater freedom of hand and arm movements. Using bar 41 as an example, the first three notes are played with 5-2-1 and then the hand is moved laterally, placing the fifth finger on the next note (G). The rest of the notes now lie under the hand.

There are some beautiful enharmonic shifts in the harmony, such as in bars 34 and 36; time will be needed for these, so a sensitive ear for colour and some rubato are essential. The two-against-three rhythm (bars 44, 46 etc.) needs to sound relaxed and smooth, and look out for the change back to simple quavers in bar 71. The arpeggiated chords at the end will need extra practice as the melody notes are inside the chords, not at the top. Initially roll the chords slowly, aiming the weight at the melody notes and keeping the others very quiet. These harp-like chords and the key of E major (one of Liszt's favourite effects) suggest a mood of heavenly bliss after the melancholy and stress of E minor.

Although there are technical challenges, the music is so beguiling that it is well worth the effort involved in its preparation.

B:6 Szymanowski *Prelude in D flat*

The nine preludes of Op. 1 were written while the young Polish composer was still in his teens. Inspired by Chopin, they are Romantic in character but show a growing awareness of dissonance. The third prelude is the only one written in the major mode; the rather introverted mood will suit the thoughtful pupil who enjoys something different.

Only after a look at the way the piece is constructed, though, will it begin to make musical sense. It falls into regular four-bar phrases, but Slavic speech rhythms can be heard at work here, especially in the unusual phrase-endings (e.g. at bars 4 and 8). Each phrase slows down on its last beat, rather like a chorale. To mark the end of each section (bars 8, 16 and again at the end) there is a rallentando that should be a little more drawn-out. Where a ritenuto is otherwise marked (e.g. bars 10 and 14) it should apply just to that moment and not continue into the next bar.

The texture is quite contrapuntal, but the main melody is clearly in the treble. An interesting process of metamorphosis takes place with this theme. After the first statement the second phrase begins as though to repeat the first, but changes direction about halfway through. The third manages the first few notes, the fourth only the first, but all the time the same rhythmic pattern creates a remarkable, almost hypnotic unity. In the final section (bar 17) the melody returns to its original form, but is now accompanied by a low, tolling bell. The composer asks for this octave Ab to continue vibrating: either employ half-pedalling, or keep the pedal down through the third beat of each bar. If the *una corda* pedal is also used, the slight blurring of overlapping harmonies will create a mistiness that is quite appropriate to the style and mood.

While the right hand is mostly diatonic with only occasional accidentals, the left hand is much more chromatic. Great care will be needed over the initial note-learning, and separate-hands practice is advisable in the early stages. Few cautionary accidentals are added, so take each bar at face-value. For instance, in bar 5 there is a G♮, but bar 6 begins with a G♭, while in bar 13 the F♮ and F♭ occur in the same chord.

A tempo of crotchet = 63 would be suitable. With its atmosphere of quiet meditation, one could imagine this mysterious piece being sung by a cathedral choir.

C:1 Kabalevsky *Presto*

Kabalevsky wrote a wealth of attractive teaching pieces that are enjoyable to play while serving a real teaching purpose. The athleticism of this lively movement, which is suitable for small hands, is instantly appealing, and has the added advantage of sounding more difficult than it actually is! Your pupil might also enjoy investigating the other two movements of this sonatina, both of which are suitable for a Grade 7 player.

Good facility over the whole keyboard and well-developed finger-work are essential for a confident performance. Note-patterns are usually logical and easily learnable. For instance, the run in bars 47–9 combines a G melodic minor scale in the right hand with its arpeggio in the left; however, a few isolated bars, especially in the middle section, may need singling out for practice.

Understanding the clear-cut sonata-form construction, with its exposition of first and second subjects in bars 1 and 19 respectively, followed by a development/transition leading to the recapitulation of both subjects beginning at bar 73, will enable your pupil to gain an overview of the whole movement.

'Presto' should be regarded more as an indicator of the movement's character than as an instruction to play as quickly as possible! If the suggested metronome marking seems too brisk for comfort, a slightly slower tempo would work equally well provided that the lively mood is not compromised. Feeling the pulse in dotted crotchets is important if the rhythm is to have buoyancy, and a firm rein is needed to prevent rushing at the crescendos. In addition, there should be no change to the basic pulse when the time signature shifts to 2/4 at bars 43 and 116.

The quavers will have added definition if, as indicated, they are played detached and *non legato* – a demanding option that relies on good finger-staccato. Although the fast-moving detail renders pedal inappropriate for much of the piece, occasional dabs, as in the opening bars, will enhance the harmonies and 'point' important notes.

Structure and variety can be given to the performance by vividly contrasted dynamics. The two subjects at the outset should be clearly differentiated, with short, light left-hand chords accompanying the second, and the allargando which heralds the recapitulation will be more effective if started earlier in bar 72, as the movement reaches its loudest point thus far. The difference between tenuto lines, which often help to define the pulse, and the sharper, more percussive accents should be shown. Elsewhere the impact of the crescendos, which need careful pacing, especially on the final page, will be heightened if each one starts sufficiently quietly.

C:2 Martinů *Harlequin (Scherzo)*

This unusual piece, which explores many facets of this puppet character through movement and dance, seems at first sight to consist of a number of disparate sections. However, on closer examination, three main sections can be detected, with the opening idea reappearing at the end but transformed into a big waltz. Each section has its own distinct character and tempo, and the use of repeated patterns, a hallmark of Martinů's style, features widely throughout the piece. Good facility is needed to manage the leaps in both hands and a convincing performance will be reliant on confident characterization and a strong sense of rhythm.

The opening ten-bar section, in E♭ major (despite the lack of a key signature), comprises two phrases of equal length, the second of which echoes the first. Firm bass notes on each main beat will underpin the harmonies here as the right hand conveys puppet-like movements. The crescendos help to propel the music forwards and *con giusto* indicates the composer's wish for precise rhythmic accuracy.

A change of mood occurs at bar 11 as well-defined quavers and strong accents suggest a fanfare. All bars are divided between the hands, and rests in bars 17 and 19 require careful counting. Perhaps the puppet is in love during the more tender, dreamy *grazioso* theme, which needs a smooth, well-shaped tone, with the right-hand 3rds sounding exactly together; the pedal can be held through each bar. Bar 32 sees another repeated pattern, this time a hemiola in the right hand, which forms a quiet accompaniment for the left-hand melodic phrases. The slower harmonic rhythm at this point seems to call for less frequent pedal changes. Yet another idea emerges as the dynamic drops to *pianissimo* at bar 48. Keeping the fingers close to the keys will help to produce quiet, smooth quavers over which the right hand dreamily recalls the opening music. The *8va* signs need care as yet another pattern emerges in bar 55, and a long pause after the build-up will increase the air of expectancy.

There is a mood of grandeur and elation as the gestures of the Allegro con brio waltz encompass the whole keyboard. Rhythm needs a one-in-a-bar impetus, and the first crotchet beats in the bass, sustained by the pedal, act as a foundation for both rhythm and harmony. Memorizing the whole section could help accuracy in the leaps; the left hand here may need separate practice. The chords oscillate between E♭ and B majors at the *accel.*, and the Presto suggests the puppet running off-stage only to falter slightly as he remembers to bow on the final second-beat *sforzando* chords.

C:3 P. F. Webster and S. Burke *Black Coffee*

The atmosphere of the exam room needs to be transformed briefly to that of the night-club for this arrangement of a 1940s standard with its deliciously bluesy slow-moving harmonies and laid-back swung rhythms. 'Moody' encapsulates the style, which should be unhurried and as sensitive as the most tender of jazz vocals.

The song is in ternary form with almost identical first and last sections, thus cutting down on note-learning; sandwiched in-between is a contrasted, more upbeat middle section.

Although there is no substitute for feeling the rhythm, many pupils who are inexperienced in this idiom may need to work out the swung quaver patterns in order not to distort the rhythmic structure. However, in the end mathematics must be cast aside to allow the rhythm to flow naturally and easily. Crotchet triplets need good spacing, and whenever the opening figure (in bars 1–2) recurs the right-hand chords should be placed before, not on, the main beat. Although the accidentals may look daunting at first, understanding the way in which the patterns relate to each other will help to secure the chords in the memory – for instance, the semitone shifts in the left-hand figure in bars 3–6. Playing the chord on the fourth beat of bar 11 with the left hand will allow the right hand to hold the melody note without a change of finger.

The texture of the outer sections, with its mixture of sung phrases and accompanying vamp bars, should be clearly differentiated. The melodic lines need a subtle projection – firm yet gentle – over the chords while the more subdued, velvet-smooth vamp bars will allow the tied melodic notes at the ends of phrases to be heard clearly. Legato pedalling, as indicated, will sustain the harmonies, and care is needed to ensure that bass notes are caught at each change. Elsewhere the ear is the best guide to the amount of pedal to use – for instance, pedal will enhance the subtlety of the opening bars whereas the triplets in bar 7 may be best left unpedalled.

The slightest hint of moving forwards at bar 26 seems to suit the more upbeat feel to the eight-bar middle section. The rhythm is more straight-forward here, apart from bar 32 which will need care; again, the melodic notes should be well to the fore, especially as the song reaches its climax at bars 31–3. Some of the widely spaced chords may be redistributed between the hands, the lowest note being played with the left thumb if more comfortable, and all harmony notes should be sustained by the pedal when spreading chords.

C:4 Gershwin *'S Wonderful*

This feel-good music with its easy two-in-a-bar lilt and charm is bound to bring a smile to the examiner's face. A large hand is an obvious advantage in negotiating the left hand's chords and patterns over a wide spread; however, pupils with a smaller stretch should not be put off sampling this delight, and can on occasion omit a less crucial note in the chord.

The piece – in ternary form, with the main climax in the eight-bar middle section – is only 32 bars long and yet it contains a number of tricky passages and many accidentals which need close scrutiny. Practising the first section with the left hand alone – using dabs of pedal (in addition to the marked pedalling) to highlight main beats and slurs – will develop the ease of movement that is so fundamental to this style. Understanding the relationship between adjacent chords also helps the learning process; for instance, in bar 6 all three notes in the left-hand chord shift down a semitone, and many notes remain stationary in bars 21–4.

Gershwin himself was a fine pianist and the writing reflects his own facility and attention to detail. Phrasing is clearly indicated with accents, tenuto marks and rhythmic detail, leaving the player in no doubt about the composer's intentions.

The tone is predominantly gentle and coaxing in the opening section, yet the cross-phrasing and accentuation lend excitement and playfulness at times. The stronger mood of the middle section is prepared by the crescendo in bars 15–16 and the pedalling here serves to emphasize the irregular phrasing. Little or no pedal will allow clarity and definition to the quaver chords in bars 17–20, which should be played unswung and with well-projected accents. A slight forward momentum will enhance the feeling of elation at this point, only to be drawn back at the *fortissimo* climax. Careful voicing of the chords in bars 21–4 will highlight the chromatic shifts, and sonority will be added by generous use of the pedal.

At the final section an ascending quaver figure transports the music of the opening to new heights. The rhythm in bar 28 needs precision and the glissando must be accurately paced in order not to arrive too early at the top. The penultimate bar should sound effortless as it draws the piece gently to a close. Practising the awkward shapes of this bar in four separate block-chord positions, using the suggested fingering, will help to secure the notes under the fingers.

C:5 Stephen Hough *Valse enigmatique No. 2*

A heady mix of the French ballroom and sounds from the Orient seems to pervade this delightful waltz by one of the UK's best-known pianists. The alternation of languorous movement in the 'Tempo rubato' phrases and the more strictly rhythmic figures form the backbone of much of the piece, while a faster middle section gives an airy lightness through its delicate textures and regular crotchet movement.

The music lies comfortably under the fingers, provided that the player is able to negotiate the changes of register over the whole keyboard. Accidentals need close attention; some are used to effect a brief excursion to a new key, while others (e.g. in bars 37–8) serve to produce an almost Ravelian harmonic frisson. (Note that the first full bar in this edition is, unusually, bar 2.) The G♯ in bar 5 must not be mistaken for F♯, a common error in note-reading. Fingering the right hand's 4ths in pairs, using either 5/2, 4/1 or 5/2, 3/1 as appropriate, will allow these figures to flow easily. The final ascending quaver arabesques need reliable fingering: placing the thumb immediately after the black note as the quavers ascend will work well.

The tempo in the rubato phrases should be unhurried, giving time to enjoy the melodic shapes and colourful harmonic changes. The 'Tempo giusto' bars, however, move along more briskly, yet with an increasingly warm tone in the leisurely *sostenuto* bars. While much of the piece is delicate and veiled, the *forte* as the tonality briefly reaches G♯ minor at bar 31 is a moment to play with real warmth and sonority. The pedal, which can be often held through the bar, contributes much to the harmonic hues of these outer sections.

Lateral movement of the hand, swinging towards the top note, will facilitate a smaller hand to negotiate with ease the left hand's 10th chords in the middle section, in addition to enabling the upper melodic notes to feature more prominently. The tempo can be slightly faster at this point, with the accompanying *pianississimo* crotchets moving as delicately as possible as they accompany the left hand with bell-like clarity. Most candidates will elect to use the pedal to sustain the chords here, in which case skill is needed to catch all three notes at each change. The *calando* at bar 75 allows the pace to unwind for the return to the opening mood. The *quasi cadenza* quavers need good facility and safe patterning in order to achieve a throw-away effect, before the final enigmatic chord – enhanced by the sustained As from the previous bar – creates an air of mystery.

C:6 Poulenc *Le petit éléphant*

This delicious extract from a work for piano and narrator depicts Babar, that lovable elephant-about-town, as he proudly takes a leisurely stroll in his new suit. The overall mood is dreamy and sophisticated with a wash of Impressionist elegance, yet with an almost balletic quality to its café-waltz rhythm.

Although not used here, Poulenc's familiar instruction 'avec beaucoup de pédale' could easily be applied to this piece, for the pedal is essential for creating a rich harmonic blanket over which the right hand spins its delicate arabesques. Releasing the pedal once per bar works well for much of the time, and only the bars with a faster harmonic rhythm need more frequent changes. The crotchet pulse should feel relaxed, elastic even, but rhythmic detail should be precisely observed within the pulse, especially the dotted and double-dotted quavers. However, the arpeggios that finish each half of the piece must be played with all the nonchalant charm and ease of the most suave cocktail pianist.

Care is needed to ensure that the clef changes in both hands are correctly observed. The frequent accidentals in this essentially Ab major tonality require both a keen eye and a feel for the idiomatic harmonies. Notice, for example, that the outer left-hand notes in bar 9 remain stationary while only the middle note shifts upwards by a semitone. The span of the *8va* sign in bars 7–8 also needs care. The left hand should pass effortlessly over the right at times, and the seemingly eccentric repeated use of the third finger in the descending chromatic runs (if obeyed) will create just the right amount of attack on the accents. Note also that the left-hand dotted minims at the start of bar 15 should be an octave A♭.

Poulenc supplied few dynamic clues for the first half of the piece, but an atmosphere of delicacy and charm must pervade this section, with the left hand always acting as accompanist. Bars 7–10 are effective when played more quietly than the opening, with the *8va* figures no more than a whisper; the *una corda* pedal can be used here and in other *pianissimo* bars to create a subtle, veiled tone quality. The two *forte* interjections (bars 15 and 18) which evaporate should come as something of a shock (did Poulenc intend both of these phrases to end *pianissimo*?). Each semi-quaver accent needs clear definition and the player must allow the pulse to stretch to accommodate the rhythmic detail – one must never feel rushed in this piece! The *mezzo-forte* phrase that follows adds a seriousness to the proceedings – notice that the right hand's second-inversion chords rise chromatically in semitones – before the force once more evaporates to end the piece in a calm, dream-like state.